Network Concepts and Architectures

Network Concepts and Architectures

Bill Hancock

QED Information Sciences, Inc.
Wellesley, Massachusetts

Ethernet is a trademark of Xerox Corporation

DEC, DECnet, DECServer, DECUS, DELNI, DEUNA, DEQNA, DEL-QA, DELUA, DEMPR, DEREP,DEBET, PDP, VAX, VAXCluster, VAX/VMS, VT and the Digital Logo are trademarks of Digital Equipment Corporation

3Com, 3Plus, EtherSeries, EtherPlus, 3Server are trademarks of 3Com Corporation

Excelan is a trademark of Excelan Corporation

Macintosh is a trademark licensed for use to Apple Computer

MS-DOS and MS-NET are trademarks of Microsoft Corporation

PC Network, IBM, IBM PC, Personal System/2, and the IBM Logo are trademarks of International Business Machines

PDS is a trademark of American Telephone and Telegraph

Wins is a trademark of the Wollongong Group

International Standard Book Number: 0-89435-270-9
Printed in the United States of America
89 90 91 10 9 8 7 6 5 4 3

Library of Congress Cataloging-in-Publication Data

Hancock, Bill, 1957–
    Network concepts and architectures.

    1. Computer networks.   2. Computer network architectures.   I. Title.
    TK5105.5.H36   1988   004.6   88-32099
    ISBN 0-89435-270-9 (alk. paper)

Contents

Chapter One - What is Communication?   1

Chapter Two - The Basics   9

Chapter Three - Communication Hardware Concepts   35

Chapter Four - Network Design, Analysis, & Politics   53

Chapter Five - Network Architecture   77

Chapter Six - Dial-up Networking   89

Chapter Seven - The Local Area Network Experience   101

Chapter Eight - Digital Network Architecture   133

Chapter Nine - Systems Network Architecture   147

Chapter Ten - Transmission Control Protocol/Internet Protocol   157

Chapter Eleven - Network Encryption   173

Chapter Twelve - Office Automation Networks   179

Chapter Thirteen - Selecting Network Consultants   193

Chapter Fourteen - Distributed Database Issues   203

Chapter Fifteen - Network Training   213

Foreword

The idea for this book resulted from one of my very frequent trips to the bookstore. Upon inspection of the various titles on networking and data communications, I failed to find any straightforward books on computer networking or descriptions of the various types of network architectures. While it is true that there were a few titles on the subject of networking, many were on how to use the various timesharing services or theoretical aspects of data communications. I could not find any books on general network concepts. Worse, I found very little intelligible information on the various types of network architectures and where they are applicable in the area of computer networking. Not that there are not good books on networking — there are. Many, however, are too general or too technical. There are few in the middle.

During further conversations with various friends in the industry, I was told that they were having a tough time explaining to their management about how computer networks and computer network architectures work and the difficulties involved with such projects. Many managers and nontechnical personnel do not fully appreciate the issues and problems involved in computer networking including design, preparations, installation, and many other issues having to do with computer networks. Not that they don't want to know — the problem is where to go for information.

This book is not the end-all solution for understanding network concepts and architectures. Its purpose is to enlighten the reader on concepts, buzzwords, and topics involved with various aspects of computer networking.

I hope that you enjoy this book. If you have some comments on how this book could be improved, please feel free to contact me at P.O. Box 13557, Arlington, Texas 76094-0557.

Bill Hancock
5/1/88

Acknowledgments

In any undertaking, there are always many individuals who help keep things on track.

First, I need to thank my reviewers: Bill Brindley of the U.S. Navy, Mike Heagney of Marathon Oil International, Sandy Traylor of Target Systems, Jim Ebright of Software Results Corporation, and Ken O'Mohundro of Able Computer. Their comments and insight of the various chapters reviewed was most valuable and enlightening.

I also need to thank Brindley McGowan of Hughes Aircraft for technical support and friendship during the production of this book.

As always, my friend and colleagues at ERI Training, Marty Davis, Bob Branchek, Bob Russo, Fred Sanders, Jill Davis, and Debbie Amiel were their usual highly helpful and professional selves, critical to the production and marketing of this book.

Finally, my thanks to those of you who have purchased this book. I hope that you will find it enlightening, entertaining, and useful in your network endeavors.

Chapter One

What Is Communication?

INTRODUCTION

"Communication is, son, what you will get across your posterior if you do not clean up your room!"

How about this one:

"I mean, like, you know, like, there was just no communication between us, man. We were on this really weird trip and just couldn't seem to reach the same line pattern; y'know what I mean?"

Of course, there's always this one:

"Thank you for your letter of 9 October. In response, we would like to ascertain the relationship, through differential and qualitative thought, of our mutual and underlying interests regarding the manner in which your office plans to concatenate and otherwise perform an overall and lasting modification of corporate guidelines to reduce the amount of unnecessary and verbose correspondence between office hierarchies."

Finally, we've all heard this one:

"The check is in the mail."

What we have just seen is proof that humans do not communicate properly. In the course of everyday life, we all are faced with instances where communication "breaks down." We are then forced to consider alternative means of communication such as different patterns of speech, reiteration of verbal communication, or even to communicate our desires and displeasures through an alternative communications media, such as physical actions (sign language, body motions, physical violence). This book is not about how people talk to people; more it is how people talk to machines (computers) and how machines talk to other machines. It is important, however, to understand that people build machines, sometimes in our own image and likeness. As a result, many different types of computing systems and data communication procedures have developed, often leading to a breakdown in communications.

The Human-Machine Experience

There was a time when communicating with computing machines was difficult. Anyone desiring access to the all-powerful computer had to first fill out countless request forms (computer cards) and present them to the computer's representative, the batch stream operator. The operator would then tell the luckless user that they would be ready soon. How soon? "As soon as they are ready!"

Oh.

After waiting a reasonable amount of time, the user would return to the all-powerful computer and ask the operator for the data requested. One of two responses seemed to be the most common in those days: "Sorry, it's not ready yet," or, "What job?"

Realizing that batch computing was slow and produced results that were often not timely, the term "interactive systems" soon became the cry of system purchasers and users worldwide. With an interactive system, users would have use of a terminal to communicate directly to the all-powerful computer and have it execute programs interactively with the user. This led to many users being able to perform work more quickly and efficiently, as well as giving them control over the all-powerful computer. But, with all good things, problems must arise.

2

More terminals began to appear on systems, meaning that more data was being required more often by more users for management decision making and for everyday production. Soon it became apparent that the computers purchased would not be able to handle the amount of terminals that were being added to them. This led to a general user revolt, in some companies, because there were "never enough terminals" to do work on and the computer system could not support more.

Users were then lured by the prospect of the personal computer (PC). The idea of computing on one's desk was very attractive as was the ability to not have to beg for computer time from the all-powerful computer or surly operators. With PCs, computing could be done by the user, for the user, and without, necessarily, the help of the computer types. With the introduction of user-usable (I avoid the term user-friendly, as most programs are not) programs, spreadsheets, and databases, the ability to effectively use the PC as a serious business tool became viable. Unfortunately, the need did not alleviate the load on the all-powerful computer and a new need surfaced at the same time: getting information between PCs and the all-powerful computer in an easy, efficient manner.

On the other side of data processing were the engineering and scientific communities, who desired the use of computing systems for precise calculations and for other functions such as numerical control, process control, computer-aided design (CAD) and computer-aided manufacturing (CAM). Where computing within the commercial environment tolerated some delays in generation and collection of data, in the engineering and scientific environments minor deviations in measurements or time can be critical to operations. As a result, engineering and scientific programs tend to be more compute-intensive (i.e., making exhaustive use of central processing unit resources) rather than I/O-intensive (making exhaustive use of input-output related peripheral devices, such as disk drives).

Most commercial data processing shops utilize the batch-oriented or interactive ("timesharing" — every user shares an equal amount of time) computing systems, which were designed for I/O operations and also for multiple terminal requests from users. These two types of computing systems are, unfortunately, inadequate for engineering and scientific operations. This led to the development of what is called "real-time" systems. Real-time systems respond to nebulous items called "events." An event could be the completion of an I/O request, and interruption of the system by an analog collection device, power failure, etc. Essentially, it is important to know that an event is, simply, anything that has the potential of changing the status of the system. Through the use of event-oriented systems, engineers and scientists could now design systems to manage operations that required real-time (immediate) response and action: manufacturing, assembly, chemical reaction control, nuclear reaction and fission control, process control, and many other items. To develop such systems, however, the scientific and engineering personnel needed much more sophisticated development environments than the classic commercially-oriented developer. Problems such as display graphics, flow mechanism, exacting display graphics for computer-aided design, simulation of electrical circuitry and many other high-power consumption needs forced the development of engineering workstations.

Engineering workstations are used for a variety of tasks, but usually in the areas of computer-aided design (CAD), computer-aided manufacturing (CAM), and computer-aided engineering (CAE). With the influx of CA-oriented workstations has also come the problem of high-speed communications and sharing of data and programming. CA-oriented stations tend to use very powerful PCs, minicomputers, or superminicomputers to provide the compute power necessary to handle the graphics, math-intensive computations, database access, and communications needs of the modern CA-oriented workstation. Along the lines of the CA-oriented workstation is a new line of workstations called computer-aided programming (CAP) stations that are used by programmers and systems personnel to produce sophisticated computer applications through non-traditional means. CAP stations can provide interactive Artificially Intelligent (AI) environments for AI programming, graphic display meta-environments for graphics programming, programming tools and programmer-friendly symbolic debugging systems. As with the commercial environment, however, the need for communications between engineering workstations and the all-powerful computer (as well as amongst each other) are increasing and the technology is not keeping up with the demand.

As it can be seen, the human-machine interface can be very complex indeed. The way that a personnel specialist communicates with a computer system and the way that an engineer communicates with a computer system can be radically different due to the nature of the job at hand and also the type of computer that is used to perform the job.

The Machine-Machine Interface

If you think that getting humans to communicate with each other is tough, try to get two dissimilar computing systems to "talk" to each other. It is very similar to an American attempting to communicate with a Chinese without either having knowledge of the other's language, customs, and idioms. Needless to say, the attempt at verbal communication is doomed to be worthless, and gestures between the two can sometimes do more harm than good. For example, consider the gesture that most Americans use to indicate the number two — the index and middle finger extended, the rest of the fingers folded, usually with the back of the hand towards the person the gesture is directed at. For most of us, this indicates two (2) of something: hamburgers, french fries, soft drinks, hurricanes, H-bombs, demolition derbys, ad infinitum. Now, just for excitement, travel to Scotland, walk into the local pub, and order two beers using the same gesture. Do not be surprised if the bartender attempts bodily harm on you! The same gesture that indicates two of something in the United States means, basically, "up yer kilt, laddie" in Scotland. The point is that frequently, we humans can communicate with sign language and get results (desirable or undesirable), even though we may not understand the language of the other person we are attempting to communicate with.

Computing systems do not have the luxury of being able to gesture to other computer systems when the language barrier exists. Computers, you see, are very dumb. After all, all they do is add. Ah, but you say, that's not true. Of course it is. Subtraction is the complement of addition, multiplication and exponentiation are just a bunch of adds, and division is subtractions. Even though the basic unit of work (addition) is the same in virtually every computing system, the results are different and the methods of communicating results to peripheral devices and humans tends to be unique to the computing system that created the results. Since computers cannot gesture very well, it is highly unlikely that one computer, say an IBM system, that expects to communicate in a certain manner will be able to communicate with a dissimilar computer (e.g., an Apple II).

PUTTING IT ALL TOGETHER

What does this mean? Essentially, for computers to communicate with each other, they must have something in common, like a "language" or, more specifically, a protocol. Just like there is protocol at a very formal dinner engagement that we humans might attend, computers expect a very formal protocol so that they can communicate with each other on an efficient basis. It is the job of the engineers and programmers to develop protocols so that computers can "talk" to other computers, terminals, peripherals, and humans. In case you have not met one before, those are the people who sit in their offices and cubicles, speak in unintelligible three and four letter words that no one but engineers and programmers understand, think that users are dumb, consume great deals of caffeine-laced coffee, work odd hours, and are generally considered to be somewhat strange by most users. Most of them will not byte (pun intended) if they are carefully fed massive quantities of junk food and technical publications. They are the creators of the all-elusive protocol, each with their own method of implementation and their own ideas of "what a protocol should be." This is why there is such a veritable plethora of protocols in existence and also why so many of them are incompatible with each other. Still, there are a few engineers and programmers that understand more than one type of protocol. This special type of person is the one who develops the "black box" or protocol emulator that is used for computer-computer communications. The emulator is usually a device or software program(s) that is used to "translate" one protocol into another. The idea is similar to the use of an interpreter that speaks English and Chinese. Now the Chinese can communicate with the American and the American with the Chinese. With the use of the interpreter, the two individuals now have something in common — the interpreter. In computer-computer communications, the thing in common would be the protocol emulator or the device that was developed to "interpret" communications between the two machines.

Conclusions and Warnings

It is obvious that communications between computing systems are similar in many respects to interpersonal communications between humans. There is a certain, set procedure in which communications are established, how long they continue, and (usually) a means to terminate communications. While humans communicate in languages, we frequently resort to gestures to emphasize our points or to clarify our communication to other humans. Since computers do not have this luxury, they have to be doubly specific when communicating with each other. Also, just as we know when we do not hear something quite right, we ask for it to be repeated. Computers have to do the same. We can therefore conclude that machine-to-machine communications are similar, in many respects, to human communications, the exception being that they are less tolerant than humans and cannot be physically expressive.

It is the wise implementer that understands the needs of the users and system before implementation of any computer-computer communications scheme. It also should be noted that communications are not a "quick and dirty" process. Careful thought and consideration has to be given to all aspects of pending implementations. Computers cannot do that; humans have to. This also means that implementation of any communications system will not be without expense: be prepared to reach deep into the proverbial wallet when considering communications.

Finally, consider the following diagram:

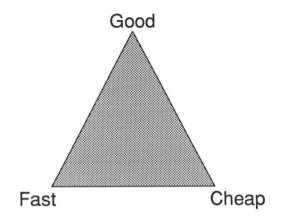

The diagram illustrated is called "Truman's Triangle," after its inventor Truman Reynolds. Think of "Truman's Triangle" as the guide to implementation of anything that is data processing related. Its use is simple: pick any two corners, such as "CHEAP" and "GOOD." You will notice that the remaining corner has the word "FAST" in it. What this means is that if you want something good and cheap, it will not be fast. In the example of the corners "FAST" and "GOOD," the result will not be "CHEAP."

Plan your communications implementation carefully. Do not be shocked when costs are uncovered — data communication is NOT cheap. Do not rush into data communications. If communications are planned and implemented correctly, they will save you time and money. If they are implemented incorrectly, do the following:

1. Be prepared to spend more to correct problems.
2. Learn to like communications downtime.
3. Stock up on your favorite ulcer medicine and aspirin.
4. Remove all sharp objects from your office.

Chapter Two

The Basics

INTRODUCTION

Understanding data communications is much like trying to learn a new language and culture at the same time. The language part involves the learning curve the newcomer to data communications experiences when trying to decipher all the bits and pieces of jargon that entwine the communications world — DDCMP, BiSYNC, ATLP's, EIA-232D, OSI, ISO, X.25, etc. Culture is something that is developed over a period of time; it involves learning to UNDERSTAND WHY equipment does what it does, protocols work the way they do, users cause the trouble they do, managers don't understand about the $1000.00 per month MODEM, and the like.

There are people who spend their lives in search of the perfect protocol — the one that allows perfect communication between everything and everyone. Others spend their lives trying to create more abbreviations for communications in hopes of reducing the overall length of communications terms. But, by and large, most of us just want to know enough to get our communications working, enhance them when they need it, keep them from breaking down, and find a way to fix our communications problems when they arise. To do this, we must understand some of the jargon of the communications world and also the basics of how to communicate.

DISTRIBUTED PROCESSING AND NETWORKING

One of the most renown problems in the communications industry is the confusion between distributed processing and networking. They ARE

NOT the same! Distributed processing refers to a managerial technique that is used to distribute a data processing workload amongst several locations or internal corporate divisions. An example would be the use of a mainframe system to perform most of the corporate processing and word processors, strategically placed throughout the organization, being used for local word processing and preliminary data collection. It is important to note that there is no direct communication between the mainframe and the word processing systems; still, distributed processing has been implemented. Computing machinery necessary for corporate operations has been distributed to the appropriate levels and users for maximum effectiveness of available resources.

Networking is the proverbial horse of a slightly different color. Networking is somewhat like distributed processing — the systems communicating may or may not be co-located, and they are probably distributed to the appropriate levels of user necessity. The difference here is that the systems actually "talk," or communicate, with each other. The communication usually involves electronic data transfer of some type over a private cable, leased cable, or public phone line. While the implementation of distributed processing concepts may be cheaper, they do not have the power of a network, or the problems. Networked systems have protocol compatibility problems, line failures, growth problems, and myriad other problems much too lengthy to be discussed at this time. For the purposes of this book, we will not discuss the usefulness of classical distributed processing; rather, we will discuss networks and networking. An understanding of networks and networking will make distributed processing techniques easily apparent.

Network Topology

Network topology is the basic outlay or design of a computer network. Think of topology as the architectural drawing of the network components, which is much like the architectural drawing of a home or building (some are simple, some are very complex). This design can be varied in accordance with the company's needs, but certain base elements to configuring the topology of a network still apply.

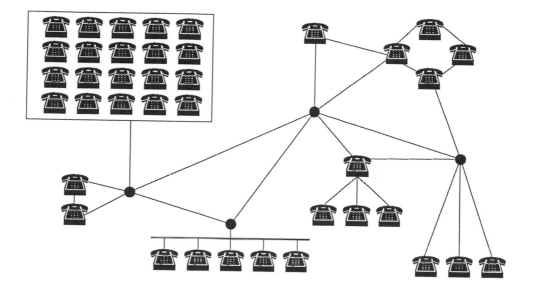

Typical Communications Topology

First off, any system on a network is called a node. Nodes are connected
to each other by things called links. Links can be phone lines, private
lines, satellite channels, etc. When you draw a roadmap of the communications links between nodes, you then have a network topology.

While we are on the subject of links, you will hear of two basic types of
links: physical and virtual. For those not familiar with the concept of vir-
tuality, the following may be helpful:

> If you can see and touch it, it's **PHYSICAL**;
> If you can see it but not touch it, it's **VIRTUAL**;
> If you can't see it and can't touch it, it's **GONE**.

Networks use virtual links to allow the sharing (multiplexing) of the physical line by multiple network programs and data transfers. If a new physical line had to be installed for every new network program that was started
up, it would be VERY expensive to provide communications capability to

many locations. Therefore, virtual communications over physical lines are extremely valuable to providing cost-effective communications capabilities.

Basic Network Topologies

Depending on the processing needs of an organization, different types of networks may be needed, sometimes even in the same organizations. There are two basic types of network models that describe most networks in existence today: point-to-point and multipoint (or multidrop).

Point-to-Point

A Point-to-Point Communications Link

Point-to-point nodes only communicate with an adjacent node — one that is "next" to the system. It should be observed that just because two systems are not in the same room, that does not mean that they cannot be adjacent. In its basic form, a point-to-point network is two nodes directly connected. In its advanced forms, it could be 200 nodes connected to adjacent nodes and those nodes connected to other adjacent nodes, ad infinitum. While not visually like the simple model of two nodes directly connected, it is still the same concept.

In the realm of Local Area Networks (LANs), many networks, while allowing a lot of nodes to communicate with each other on the same physical wire or fiber, actually look like point-to-point links. Consider, for instance, Ethernet (a variant of which is the IEEE 802.3 LAN standard). Ethernet allows up to 100 nodes (systems) per segment of cable, and each segment of cable can be up to 500 meters long. A total length of interconnected Ethernet segments cannot exceed 2.5 km.

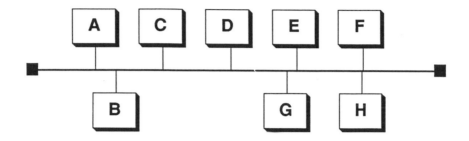

A Typical Single Segment Ethernet

Due to the nature of the Ethernet protocol and method of access, while there are multiple nodes on the network, they still look adjacent to each other. Adjacency is usually measured by how many "hops" it takes to get from the home node to the destination node. Adjacent nodes, those nodes logically ONE HOP from each other, comprise a point-to-point connection (one hop = two nodes directly connected). In Ethernet, all nodes are one logical hop from each other. Therefore, all nodes on an Ethernet are adjacent and appear to be a point-to-point topology, although, in reality, there are many nodes connected to the same physical wire.

When considering point-to-point topology, it is important to understand that the concept of point-to-point communications has changed over the last few years and that just because there is more than one node on the same physical wire does not mean that the basic topology is not point-to-point.

Routing

On some vendor's networking products, the concept of routing is introduced. Routing is the ability of a node to relay a message to another node, even though the router may not be connected directly to the node that will receive the message. The addition of routing to a network makes it much less susceptible to data loss and also reduces overall communications costs.

In the next figure we see three nodes: New York, Denver, and San Francisco. We also notice that each node has connecting lines to the other two. On systems with simple networking capability, the only way to implement communications between the nodes is in this manner. If the link between any of the two nodes goes down, the nodes cannot communicate with each other. This causes data to back up at the two nodes and create overall congestion. Another problem is that the communications costs get quite expensive — roughly $1000.00 per month per 1,000 miles. Whether the link is up or down does not matter to Ma Bell's accounting department, especially if the problem is yours. While this type of network is functional and will get the basic job done, it can be wasteful of resources.

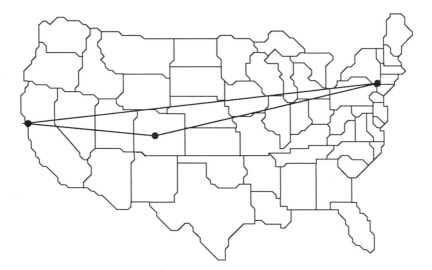

Initial Routing Configuration

Now, let's use the same setup, only this time with routing capability. If the link between New York and Denver should go down, New York simply routes its traffic through San Francisco. While this looks like the long way around, it is much better than waiting to send data because of a down line and, on most implementations of routing, the routing is transparent to the user. This type of configuration is very useful where high network

14

reliability is necessary. Most vendor implementation of this type of routing is termed alternate routing — the ability of the network software to sense that a line is down and find another way to get to the remote node.

Routing networks also have a few other redeeming qualities. If the above configuration were modified so that there was just one link from New York to Denver, and one from Denver to San Francisco, the overall link engineering is reduced, as would be the cost. With this type of configuration, routing is practically a necessity. The New York node would send a piece of data, or packet, to the Denver node with an address on it for San Francisco. The Denver node would scan the address and see if the packet was for Denver. Since it was not, the Denver node would forward the packet to the San Francisco node. This is called route-thru capability. Another feature is called load-sharing adaptive routing. This type of routing allows the systems to determine the load on a link (or links) and adjust the flow of traffic to other links to offload congested links. One or all of these features (and others) may be found in a vendor's networking products.

Depending on how the point-to-point network is configured, it can have different names, but the basic model still remains. When considering the point-to-point approach, check into the vendor's network routing capabilities prior to final acceptance of a network implementation plan. If the routing capabilities are good and the requirement for immediate throughput of data does not exist, you may be able to reduce the number of links and save your company money. Do not, however, trade money for performance. As users find out how wonderful networking is, the network gets used more and performance will suffer. Plan for this; it will happen.

Multipoint or Multidrop

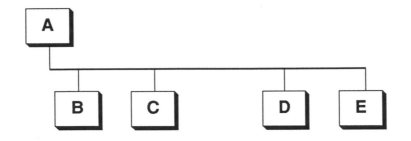

A Multidrop Network Topology

A multipoint or multidrop network is one where nodes share one line by sharing time on the line. It is very similar to the rural telephone party lines that still exist in parts of the United States today. A user picks up the line and checks to see if someone is there. If so, he hangs up and tries again later. If the line is clear, he dials the number he wishes to talk to and communication begins. Multipoint networks are very useful where high-speed data transmission capabilities are NOT necessary and where cost of implementation is a factor. Many companies that use systems to automate their production, such as breweries, run their own wires throughout the production area. If the company had to run a separate set of wires to every machine, the cost could get prohibitive very quickly. By using multipoint communications, however, the company can implement a functional network of production systems quickly and without major cost considerations. Remember that multipoint does not lend itself well to high-speed data communications, nor where there is a great volume of communications. Also, as is obvious, the more nodes on the trunk, or party, line, the more the chances of some other node communicating when the need to communicate arises. Thus, it will take longer to get the data to other systems.

Multidrop communications use a variety of methods to communicate, but two methods are dominant: the "party line" concept we saw before and the

16

master-slave concept. In the master-slave concept, one processor is called the network master and all other processors are slaves. In this method, the master controls the network functions and the slaves will request network access from the master. Should the master go down, usually one or more of the slaves will be designated as alternate network masters and take control of the network should the master go down for an inordinate amount of time.

When looking at multidrop topologies, remember that there are different methods of access and you should be very familiar with the access method before you decide if the network hardware/software fits your needs.

Ring

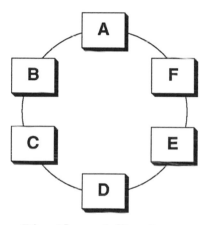

Ring Network Topology

Classic ring topologies consist of nodes arranged in a ring pattern. Data is passed between the source node and the destination node by putting the data on the ring and passing the data from node to node until the destination node receives the data. If the rotation direction were counterclockwise, to get from node A to node D, the data must travel through node B and node C. When the data packet arrives at node D, the destination node, the system removes the data and the packet is now ready for use by another node.

How data is transferred between nodes varies from ring architecture to ring architecture. Some rings transfer data in a circle rotating single-directionally in a clockwise method. Others transfer single-directionally in a counterclockwise method. Still others utilize two rings, one clockwise and another counterclockwise, and put the same data on both rings simultaneously, thus always allowing the data to take the shortest number of hops to the destination.

In addition to the direction of data movement, data can be transferred in a variety of methods as well. Some rings only allow one packet of data to be active on the entire ring at a given time. Others allow several packets to be active. Some have groups of packets called "slots" that are transferred node to node. Others allow only a single segment of multiple packets to be transferred from node to node. So, the amount of data and the direction of transfer will vary from ring topology to ring topology depending upon vendor architecture. Moreover, the throughput of data will vary from ring to ring depending upon the method of node-to-node transfer, the system-to-network interface, ring size, speed, data buffers, and many other factors. So, while ring networks can be very fast, they can also be very slow and difficult to configure if care is not exercised.

Star

Star network topologies come in a variety of layouts. Basically, however, there are two basic layouts: all nodes connected directly to each other via dedicated wiring or all nodes connected directly to each other via centralized wiring.

In the following figure, we see a star network with all nodes connected to each other via dedicated wiring. This method, while somewhat expensive, is fairly reliable, as it allows all nodes to be one hop away from each other and, therefore, adjacent. If routing is introduced to the network, should one of the links go down between any two nodes, data could be routed through an intermediary node.

18

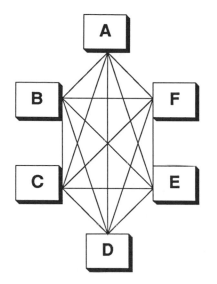

Star Network with Individual Connections

In the next figure a star network with centralized wiring is shown. In this situation, the centralized wire center is usually passive (no intelligence or power supply) and acts as a central connector for all wiring. This simplifies the wiring of the star, but introduces a potential for a single point of failure on the network. In such network topologies, there may be separate wires for each node or some sort of frequency division multiplexer (FDM) or time division multiplexer (TDM) may be used to reduce the amount of actual wire necessary for connectivity.

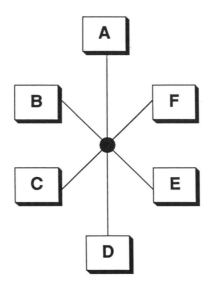

Centralized Star Topology (Utilizing a Hub)

Network Topology Summary

Networks can be configured in a variety of topologies with varying topologies interconnected with each other. There are other generalized network topologies, but understanding the basics of network topological design and some of the benefits and functions of each basic type of network allows one to visualize and understand the more complex topological networks that exist.

COMMUNICATIONS TYPES

Serial and Parallel Communications

Data can be transmitted from point A to point B in one of two basic modes: serial or parallel mode. Consider the average big city interstate freeway. Just for the sake of argument, creativity, and simplicity, let's say that the freeway is eight (8) lanes wide and that all the vehicles on it are heading east. Let's put a further stipulation that all vehicles are either red or blue and that they are all the same type.

If we close off seven of the eight lanes, we have: a) a congestion problem, and b) a general slowdown of traffic. All the vehicles have to travel one after the other in one lane with the road crews handling the congestion and making sure that everyone gets into the lane in the proper order. In other words, the vehicles are traveling serially or one after the other. Serial communications means that bits of data travel in one line, one after the other, with the system acting as the road crew to make sure that everyone gets in line in the proper place.

Now let's open up all eight lanes. If we take eight vehicles and place each one in a separate lane, side by side, they would be traveling in parallel to each other. We can also notice that in the time that it took for one vehicle to travel serially, we can have eight travel the same distance in the same time if they are traveling parallel to each other.

Since we're talking about traffic and roads, let's now look at some of the cold, hard, cash facts of road building. If we built one mile of road eight lanes wide, we could build eight miles of one-lane road for the same amount of money. Also, it is easier to get the land for single-lane roads than it is for multilane roads. Then there are the logistical problems, engineering problems, etc. The point is, the more sophisticated the solution, the more the problems and the more the cost.

What we have just been through shows serial communications — we send all the bits (ones and zeros instead of red and blue vehicles) in a single line in a certain order. We are limited to the speed of the line as to how fast we can send the bits, but we still only send one bit at a time. On a parallel communications link, we would send a group of bits at one time (the amount varies from device to device). Essentially, in the same amount of time that it would take to transmit one bit of information to the remote node over a serial line, we can transmit a byte (8 bits), word, or more data. Parallel lines have a limitation that is important to remember. The longer the parallel link, the worse the degradation of the electrical signal from the nodes farthest away. In most networking and data communications systems, parallel communications are limited to peripherals directly connected to the system and communications between systems that are physically close to each other. Serial communications are seen practically everywhere — terminals to systems, lease phone lines, dial-up lines, satellite links, etc.

Synchronous and Asynchronous Communications

Communications, in addition to being either serial or parallel, are either synchronous (sync) or asynchronous (async). It's like the saying "being in-sync with the times" — basically meaning that the person described is constantly aware of what is going on in his or her environment. If you are this type of person, you "know what is happenin', baby." If you do not, you are probably async in nature — you're not sure of what is going to happen in your environment, but you are ready for it when it does happen.

Synchronous communications mean that communications between two nodes are closely watched by each node. All actions resulting in data transmission and general link conditions are closely synchronized between the two nodes. If data is to be transmitted or received, the nodes are aware of it almost immediately and set up the exchange based on ordered data rates and sizes.

Asynchronous communications differ in that nodes don't necessarily know when data is coming to them, nor how long the data message will be. Terminals on a system are a good example of async communications. The system does not know when the terminal user will walk up to the terminal and start typing, so it has to be ready all the time.

If you are having problems differentiating the two types of communications, it is easy to compare synchronous to asynchronous when you look at them as a mugging. In the asynchronous mugging, you know you are going to be attacked, but not when (but you are always ready). In a synchronous mugging, you not only know that you are going to be mugged, but you also know when, so again, you are ready.

On most computer networks, a variety of both types of communications will be found. Most terminals, dial-up and local, are asynchronous in nature, whereas communications between systems, especially those over 2400 bits per second (baud), are synchronous. Synchronous communications tend to be more expensive than asynchronous, as the hardware involved is more costly due to integral clocking mechanisms that have to be used as well as more sophisticated engineering efforts. Yet, synchronous communication can eliminate up to 20 percent of the associated overhead inherent in asynchronous communications. This allows greater throughput of data and better error detection. Synchronous devices usually do not use START and STOP bits (described below), so coordination between the two nodes is handled differently. In synchronous communications, there are two "channels" — one for data and another for link synchronization. The "channel" for synchronization uses the integral clock in the hardware for link synchronization between the two nodes. When one of the nodes is ready to transmit data, a unique combination of bits, called a sync character, is sent to the receiver. Since the first character will probably get trashed, a second one usually follows to ensure that synchronization is complete. Systems that require two sync characters before transmission is allowed are less likely to be faked out by false noise on the line and other intangibles.

Async communications, while less expensive, have to utilize START and STOP bits to synchronize with the receiving node. Async communications lines remain in an idle state until the hardware on the line is ready to transmit. Since the line is idle (current ON), a series of bits has to be sent to the receiving node to notify it that there is data coming. When the data is finished, the node has to be notified that the transmission is complete and to go back to an idle state, hence the STOP bits. This pattern continues for the duration of the time the link is operative.

EIA and 20mA Current Loop

When considering transmission of serial data, there are two popular means by which this is accomplished: varying the current or varying the voltage.

If the current is varied, the technique is usually what is called a 20milliAmpere (20mA) current loop. The 20mA loop was designed originally for teletypes and is considered an older design, but is still found in many areas of the data processing industry. Its major benefit is that it is less susceptible to noise interference than the varying-the-voltage (EIA) technique, but its drawbacks can, on occasion, outweigh its usefulness. Drawbacks include the fact that the signal does not convey enough intelligence to support MODEMs and that there must be two types of 20mA interfaces — an active interface to supply the current and a passive interface for other devices connected in the loop. The most important drawback is the fact that since current is directly proportional to voltage and resistance, the voltage required to drive 20mA of current through the loop may be quite high. Since the voltage is frequently higher than delicate logic boards can handle, a "black box" has to be introduced to allow the transmission between the 20mA loop and the recipient device. This "black box" is called an optical isolator. Basically, an optical isolator is a light-tight box with a light source (a light emitting diode — LED) and a photo-resistor. While the 20mA current is flowing, the light is on, causing the photoresistor to react. Since the receiving unit is connected to the photo-resistor, when the reaction is active the receiver knows that a unit of information is being transmitted.

If the voltage is varied, the circuitry used to transmit the data is termed an EIA circuit. EIA stands for Electronic Industry Association, an association which drafts and defines standards for circuitry. In cooperation with the Bell System, independent MODEM manufacturers, and computer manufacturers, EIA developed a standard for the Interface between Data Terminal Equipment and Data Communication Equipment Employing Serial Binary Interchange. This standard, called EIA-232D (the D is the latest revision level) is used widely in industry and incorporates the necessary design for MODEM support. EIA interfaces transmit binary data by reversing the polarity of voltage over a direct current (dc) line. The sender transmits a positive voltage for a "0" and a negative voltage for a "1". While a much more versatile interface than the 20mA current loop, the EIA interface is much more susceptible to noise.

Transmission Modes

There are three modes of data transmission that correspond to the three types of circuits available: simplex, half duplex, and full duplex. A brief warning when reading this: even though you may be capable of communicating at full duplex, your receiver may only allow half duplex; the ensuing communications will NOT be full duplex — they will be half duplex.

Simplex

Simplex communications imply a simple method of communicating, which they are. In a simplex communications mode, there is a one-way communication transmission. Television transmission is a good example of simplex communications. The main transmitter sends out a signal (broadcast), but it does not expect a reply as the receiving units cannot issue a reply back to the transmitter.

Half Duplex

In half duplex mode, both units communicate over the same medium, but only one unit can send at a time. While one is in send mode, the other unit is in receive mode. It is like two polite people talking to each other — one talks, the other listens, but neither talks at the same time.

Full Duplex

Full duplex mode communications are interesting. Imagine two people talking at the same time and each one understanding the other perfectly. Compound that visualization with the added benefit of not having to talk about the same thing, and you have realized full duplex communications. Both sides can send and receive AT THE SAME TIME!

Parity and Error Control

In most transmission and reception systems, there is the capability to detect errors in the transmission or reception of data. The two most popular are the parity check and (mostly on synchronous communications) the Cyclic Redundancy Check.

Parity

Parity is a test that is used to detect single bit errors in transmission. Occasionally a bit gets distorted by line noise, etc., and is received incorrectly — a "1" is received instead of the "0" that was sent. Since all characters that are transmitted are represented by a unique combination of characters (seven bits for ASCII characters), this error can cause the receiver to translate the bit pattern to one that is different than the one that was sent.

Parity checking is a method used to guard against this type of error. The "1"s in a bit pattern are counted and an eighth bit (called the Parity bit — computer people are at least predictable) is set so that the total number of "1"s in the character bit pattern is EITHER EVEN or ODD. EVEN parity states that the bit will be set to make the total bit count EVEN numbered. ODD parity makes the total number of bits ODD. Occasionally, NO PARITY is seen. This means that parity is ignored altogether. For example, consider the following:

> upper case letter A = 1000001
> Total number of "1"s = 2 (an even number)
> Therefore, if EVEN parity is selected, the final bit pattern
> would be:
> > 01000001

If the parity were ODD, the final pattern would look like this:

11000001

Cyclic Redundancy Checks (CRC)

The Cyclic Redundancy Check is one of the most popular methods for ensuring the reliability of data "packets" that are transmitted to receiving nodes. Found primarily in synchronous communications, CRC is used to verify the integrity of the entire packet or block of data. In asynchronous communications, parity is frequently sufficient to ensure data integrity. In high-speed synchronous communications, however, single bit corrections are not enough. As each packet is created, a CRC check is placed somewhere in the packet (this is determined by the protocol) and is verified at the receiving end. A CRC is generated by dividing the total number of bits in the block of data being sent by a predetermined binary number. The remainder, the CRC check, is then added to the packet and the packet is transmitted. On the receiving end, the reverse mathematical operation is performed to verify the packet contents. If the computation is successful, the packet is passed to the next step. If it fails, the issuing node is notified and the entire packet is retransmitted. While a more thorough means of error detection than just parity checking, it can also be a burden. If a line is "dirty" (has a lot of noise on it), the retransmission of packets can cause line backups and overall slowdown of the data transmission throughput.

SIGNALS

Digital and Analog

All messages sent from one point to another are transmitted as either an analog signal or a digital signal, or, frequently, a little of both. Before we get too carried away as to how, we need to know what each type is.

An Example of a Digital Signal

Digital signals are what is termed discrete. Just like most computers, they are binary in nature — off or on, one or zero, etc. What makes the signal discrete is that there is no in-between. It's like a light bulb — either it's on or it's off; there is no "sort of on" or "sort of off." Therefore, we can conclude that a digital signal consists of two (and only two) states — electrical current applied or no current at all. On most systems, if power is applied, it is considered ON and usually interpreted as a "1" by the computer. If there is no power (an OFF state), the interpretation is a "0". This is called a binary interpretation and the ONs and OFFs are interpreted as BITS (1s and 0s).

An Example of an Analog Signal

Analog signals are interpreted differently. We have all seen a sine wave in basic physics; it is an electrical signal that looks like a rolling swell of water on the sea. The crest of the wave is called the peak and the depression is called the trough. How high the peaks are and how low the troughs are determine the amplitude of the signal. Each complete wavelike motion of the analog signal is called the signal's frequency. The number of cycles per second (frequency) is represented in Hertz (Hz).

Consider the act of speaking over the telephone. If we are soft-spoken, the amplitude is decreased. If we are loud, the amplitude is greater. If we speak in a high voice, the frequency changes to more cycles per second than if we spoke in a low voice, which requires less cycles. Stereo systems, television speakers, public address systems, and, most important of all, telephones are examples of analog devices.

Channels

A communications channel is the collections of links that connect the nodes of a network. To connect the nodes together, a physical medium of some kind is used, like a cable. If we want to define the total capacity of analog signals the physical media can handle, we call it the capacity rate or, more commonly, the bandwidth of the media. For example, lets say that our media was a coax cable; some varieties have a usable bandwidth of about 300 million Hz, or 3MHz (3 Mega-Hertz). That number is determined by taking the high-end frequency and subtracting the low-end frequency, yielding the bandwidth. A cable that covers the range of 10MHz to 310MHz has a bandwidth of 300MHz.

The medium selected is very important to bandwidth, and thus to communications. If a twisted-pair (two wire) cable was used instead of the coax, we would probably see bandwidths of only 1MHz to 2MHz. Fiber optics cables have a much greater capacity, usually measured in billions of Hz (GHz — Giga-Hertz).

Up to this point, bandwidth has referred only to analog communications. If we refer to bandwidth while discussing digital communications, we would be referring to the number of bits per second that could be transmitted over the channel. Local networks might offer as much as 10Mbits (Mbits — mega bits) per second; some sections of the telephone network offer 1.5M bits per second; standard phone lines have significantly lower digital bandwidths.

Signal Transmission

There are two basic ways that analog signals are transmitted over a channel: at their original frequency (a baseband signal) or combined into another signal (called a carrier) and then transmitted at a different frequency. A carrier signal is a continuous signal that is transmitted over a physical medium at a predefined frequency that is capable of being modulated (changed) to represent information.

As we pick up a telephone and speak into it, the telephone network accepts our analog voice signal at face value, but somewhere in the range of 300 to 3400 Hz. This face value acceptance is an example of a baseband signal.

Once Ma Bell has hold of the signal that we are transmitting, she does all kinds of nasty things to it. First, she uses a device called a MODEM (MOdulator-DEModulator) to create a carrier signal at a higher frequency (say, 60,000 Hz). Then, the modem takes our voice signal (still in the range of 300 to 3400 Hz) and shifts it to the range of the carrier and then transmits it to the remote station. When the signal arrives, it is demodulated by a MODEM at the remote station and the demodulated signal is passed to the receiver.

Signal Modulation

There are two main methods that can be used to perform the signal modulation previously described: frequency modulation (FM) and amplitude modulation (AM). A third method, phase modulation, is sometimes used on higher speed MODEMs and is briefly discussed below.

Frequency Modulation

Frequency modulation is when the frequency (cycles per second) of the carrier is altered to conform to the message signal, while the strength or amplitude of signal is kept constant.

Amplitude Modulation

In the case of amplitude modulation, the amplitude (strength) of the carrier signal is altered with time, to conform to the message signal, while the frequency remains constant. .

Phase Modulation

In phase modulation, the phase angle of the carrier wave is modified, affecting the frequency, while the amplitude remains constant. The changes in phase angle are what convey the information in a phase modulated signal. It should be noted that on higher speed MODEMs, a phase modulated signal and amplitude modulated signal are used to digital signals to reduce congestion and ensure proper phase angle interpretation.

Multiplexing

Multiplexing is a technique used to divide a single communications channel up into various channels to transmit a number of independent signals. Multiplexing is an important communications concept as most communications systems use some method of multiplexing and, with the extensive use of fiber communications and satellite communications, the use of multiplexing technologies will increase exponentially over the next few years. There are basically four different types of multiplexing: space, frequency, time, and demand.

Space Division Multiplexing

Probably the most inefficient of all multiplexing techniques, space division multiplexing involves the creation of a single channel by grouping together many physical channels. An example is the standard home phone system. Each house has a wire assigned to it that later joins a master cable assembly (group of wires). Each wire then has its own space in the master assembly, or, the space has been multiplexed to accommodate the wires.

Frequency Division Multiplexing

Frequency division multiplexing involves dividing the available transmission frequency range into narrower bands, each of which is used as a separate channel. You will notice that no mention was made of equal frequency ranges. The idea is that the main frequency is divided into appropriate sized subfrequencies, with each subfrequency being "tailor-made" to the bandwidth of data that it must carry. This makes frequency division multiplexing (FDM) very efficient and cost effective.

An example of FDM can easily be seen in the method of broadcast that is used by television stations. The FCC allocates a frequency band for the station to use and the station subdivides this band into various parts. One channel carries engineering information for the station's technical staff; another carries the analog signal for audio reception at the television set. Still another actually carries the video signal for home television sets. What a remote unit can pick up depends on what frequency the unit is set up for. This brings up another point about FDM — it does not randomly allocate subchannels and send data. It allocates them based on the definition of hardware circuitry of the transmitting device and demultiplexes the signal in the same manner. Think of FDM as being a parallel-like signal — all the channels being sent at once.

Time Division Multiplexing

Time Division Multiplexing (TDM) is different from FDM as each node on a channel is assigned a number and given a small amount of time in which to transmit a data packet. It varies from FDM in that FDM transmits data in a parallel-like fashion while TDM uses a serial-like fashion. The amount of time that each node gets for transmission of data depends on the clocking interval of the TDM device, the amount of nodes competing, and the polling order (the order in which the nodes are requested for information).

32

Demand Access Multiplexing

Demand Access Multiplexing (DAM) is a relatively new technology to communications. If you have been watching cellular phones becoming widespread in the U.S., then you already have an idea what DAM is all about. Basically, there is a "pool" of frequency pairs that is managed by a communications "traffic cop." The traffic cop assigns pairs of communications frequencies to a requesting station: one for transmission, one for reception (that's the DEMAND part — you DEMAND a pair and, if available, you get a pair). The traffic cop then connects the two pair of frequencies to the requestor and can also connect the two frequencies to another set of frequencies, either via classic phone communications or via Radio Frequency (RF) to another mobile unit (that is the ACCESS part). When one or both stations are through, the frequencies allocated to them are deallocated and returned to the pool for other incoming requests (that's the MULTIPLEXING part). DAM is analogous to the method in which memory is allocated on virtual computers as well. A pool of memory exists for all jobs running. When a new job needs memory, it is allocated for the job and when the job is through, it is given back to the pool for usage by another job.

Chapter Three

Communication Hardware Concepts

INTRODUCTION

In the world of data communications, a knowledge of basic communication hardware types is a veritable necessity. Most of us can tell a MODEM from a cable, but can we tell MODEMS and cables from each other? Worse yet, how do we know when to use EIA and when to use a 20Ma current loop interface? In this chapter, we hope to answer these problems and describe other general types of communication hardware.

TRANSMISSION MEDIA

Transmission media is a fancy name for communication cables. Unless a signal is transmitted via radio, laser, or semaphore, it is very difficult to get data very far without cables. Let's take a look at some of the different types of media that are used and where they are used.

Twisted Pair

Twisted pair cables consist of two wires twisted together to minimize the interference created when adjacent pairs of wire are combined in multipair cable. Probably the oldest type of communications cable still in use (it was one of the original wire types used in telephone communications), it is still used for low to medium (300 to 9600 bits per second) speed data communications with terminals and similar equipment. Another usage of twisted pair cables is in process control environments where remote systems are close enough to make phone lines an expensive commodity but cheap enough to warrant running twisted pair cable to the remote units. Typical bandwidth is 1 to 2MHz.

Coaxial Cable

Coaxial cable is a very popular physical medium for communications because of its ability to support a large bandwidth with a high immunity to electrical interference with low error occurrence. It is used very widely in telephone networks, cable TV networks, etc., where the need to multiplex many channels is necessary to reduce the number of cables that have to be installed. For example, if a cable TV company needed a single cable for every color signal it wished to send, the venture would soon prove to be cost-prohibitive as well as time-consuming. Since coax cable has a bandwidth in the range of 300-400MHz, it is capable of carrying over 50 standard 6MHz color TV channels or thousands of channels of voice-grade and/or low-speed data over a single cable. With the widespread usage of coaxial cable, interfaces are plentiful and inexpensive, making it readily available and moderate in cost.

Coaxial cable is used in both baseband and broadband networks. Baseband networks are networks where the entire bandwidth of the cable is utilized for a single channel. Broadband is basically a frequency division multiplexed situation where the coaxial cable's bandwidth is separated into subchannels of either equal or varying frequency ranges that can be treated as separate communications media. While both communications mechanisms use coaxial cable, it is important to know that the method in which the cable is used is radically different in both situations. Since the usage of the coaxial cable varies greatly, the method in which the cable is set up for each type of network technology is different and, in some cases, incompatible. In other words, if the initial system that is used is based upon baseband technology, it is highly possible that conversion to broadband technology over the same coaxial cable will require a great deal of modifications to the existing cable, interfaces, and other considerations.

Optical Links

Optical links are made of plastic or glass and have the potential of being a very high performance transmission medium under certain conditions.

The reasons for this are obvious:

a) Current fiber-optic cables can support up to 3.3 billion Hz (3 giga-Hertz — 3GHz) compared to the upper end of coaxial cable, which is in the range of 500MHz
b) Low error rate, eliminating many transmission and reception error checking methods
c) Not affected by noise or electrical interference. Additionally, they do not emit noise or interference.
d) Very small in size
e) New fiber technologies allow teraHertz (trillions) bandwidths and multi-gigabit speeds

To communicate over a fiber-optic link, the electrical pulse that makes up a "1" or a "0" has to be translated into a light pulse by a light source (usually a LED or a laser diode) and detected by the receiver through a photoelectric sensor and converted to electricity again.

Signal Dispersion

The performance that is realized over a fiber-optic link is determined by the degradation or dispersion of the light signal over the fiber. This degradation affects the speed of transmission, bandwidth, and distance. On most current types of fiber-optic communications, there are two dispersion types: chromatic and modal.

Chromatic Dispersion

Chromatic dispersion is determined by the range of light wavelengths produced by the light source. The wider the range is at the source, the quicker the signal degrades. LEDs are less expensive than laser diodes, but they emit a broader range of light frequencies and can thus only achieve speeds of up to 150 mega-bits per second over one kilometer compared to the laser system, which produces 2500 mega-bits per second over the same distance.

Modal Dispersion

Modal dispersion is the tendency of light to travel in a wavelike motion, rather than in a straight line. The larger the wave fluctuations, the greater the dispersion of the signal and degradation of performance.

Fiber Types

There are three types of fibers that are available for transmission purposes. Fibers vary by different thicknesses and densities with each variety having tradeoffs between ease of use and performance. Additionally, all fibers are enclosed in an opaque material to prevent light from escaping and to prevent outside light from entering.

Single Mode

An extremely thin fiber (and not currently commercially available), single mode fibers cause light to travel in a very straight path, provide low modal dispersion, and, as such, are very high performers. The thinness of the fibers causes problems with connecting interfaces.

Stepped Index

Thicker than the single mode fiber, for ease of use, this type of fiber carries signals at lower rates (20 mega-bits per second over one kilometer) over smaller distances. It is, however, much easier to interface to and manipulate, but does have a much greater modal dispersion.

Graded Index

The most common of the three types of fibers, this fiber is more dense than the previous two. The fiber is of varied density from the inside out; this has a modulating effect on the light pulses as they disperse and forces them to travel and arrive in-sync with signals that have not yet dispersed. Faster than stepped index, but slower than single mode (speed is about 1 giga-bit per second over one kilometer), it is widely used in commercial environments.

Graded index fiber is currently the most popular fiber for interconnection of communications equipment such as Ethernet bridges, PBX systems, and many other types of equipment. The most popular in the U.S. is the 62.5 micron size.

COMMUNICATIONS LINE CONDITIONING

With the use of higher and higher speed MODEMS (described in the following section), noise and other types of interference become troublesome to communications. A one second burst of static will wipe out 30 characters on a phone line that is supporting 300 baud communications, 120 characters on a line that is supporting 1200 baud, or 960 characters on a 9600 baud line. As can be seen, the higher the speed of the line, the more important it becomes to ensure that noise and static be eliminated wherever possible. To do this, Ma Bell has come up with a series of line conditioning services, appropriately priced, for leased line (ONLY) communications links. To find out the actual prices, contact your local phone company business office.

On any phone line where communications speeds exceed 1200 baud, some type of line conditioning should be considered. How much is up to your budget and what your error tolerance levels are (if you don't care about errors, don't worry about it; if you do, determine how many you can live with). The following is a list of conditioning types extracted from AT&T technical publication PUB41004, "Data Communications Using Voiceband Private Line Channels." "Basic" infers that no conditioning is used and some of the higher speed MODEMs that are available may or may not need line conditioning due to their ability to correct errors independently.

With the advent of digital communications links and a digital phone system, the need for line conditioning is becoming less and less critical. Further, many MODEMs are beginning to implement various permutations of the Microcom Networked Protocol (MNP). Through this technique, MODEMs negotiate with each other over the best line protocol to use. Following selection, MODEM to MODEM communication proceeds utilizing the protocol and the session does not receive any errors in transmission.

Finally, a stern warning. While the first reaction may be to ignore channel conditioning (opting to install it later), the phone company changes just like any other large organization, so a line with no conditioning could degrade if a facilities change were implemented. With conditioning, the electrical quality of the line is guaranteed for Bell MODEMS (other manufacturers are not guaranteed), so such occurrences are rare. It is one of the situations you were warned about in Chapter 1 — if you make a mistake in setting up a link or in design, get ready to pay more to correct it.

MODEMs

Anyone in the data communications or data processing fields for more than five minutes has heard of MODEMS. As previously described, MODEM stands for MOdulator-DEModulator — one modulates a signal with a carrier and the other demodulates the signal back to the original form. MODEMs are used practically anywhere data communications between remote terminals and systems and remote system to system communications are found.

It is beyond the scope of this book to go into the nuts and bolts aspects of MODEMs. We will, therefore, concern ourselves with the types of MODEMs on the market, where they are used (and when), and nomenclature (where appropriate). For those interested in actual MODEM specifications and circuitry layout, contact your MODEM manufacturer. For information on AT&T MODEM standards (which most of the industry uses), contact the following:

American Telephone and Telegraph Company
Supervisor, Information Distribution Center
195 Broadway, Room 208
New York, New York 10007

All requests to this address should include billing and shipping information. Documentation that can be obtained includes the Technical Reference Catalog (PUB40000), Data Communications Using the Switched Telecommunications Network (PUB41005), Dataphone (MODEM) Interface Standards (there are different ones for different interface types), etc. To those who are technicrats, you will find them quite enlightening. To those that are not, they are better than sleeping pills.

Other types of MODEMs are CCITT-compliant. For CCITT specifications, contact the U.N. Bookstore in New York and ask for the V-series of CCITT specifications (red books).

Some MODEMs are claimed to be Hayes compatible. Hayes, a communications company in the U.S., implemented a series of user or system initiated commands that "tell" a directly connected MODEM how it should handle the communications session. The set of commands has been replicated on many MODEMs, hence the term "Hayes compatible."

How a MODEM Works...

At the risk of losing your interest, it is still worthwhile to understand the basic concepts of MODEM operation. What was, at first, a simple data communications device is becoming increasingly complex as communications technology expands. Still, most of the basic concepts still apply to most MODEMs. For the purposes of discussion, all examples will be limited to the 300 baud full-duplex MODEM and the 1200 baud half-duplex MODEM.

Half-duplex MODEMs

As previously defined in Chapter 2, a half-duplex communication mode indicates that only one side at a time can be communicating over a link. As we also remember, a voice-grade telephone line is capable of supporting a

41

frequency range of 300-3400Hz. So far, so good. On a half-duplex MODEM, the "1"s and "0"s (or MARKs and SPACEs) are transmitted to the receiver at different frequencies within the available frequency range. This type of transmission is called Frequency Shift Keying (FSK). This means that when the MODEM is transmitting and detects a "1", it transmits at a frequency of 1200Hz (MARK). If a "0" is detected, a pulse on frequency 2200Hz is sent (SPACE). Another feature of some MODEMs is what is called a reverse channel. The reverse channel on the Bell 202 type of MODEMs is at frequency 387Hz and is used by the receiving station to notify the transmitting station that the data being sent is being received. By using this method of checking, this eliminates the need for half-duplex MODEMs to issue a read on the line after every send to see if there is a need to relinquish the line to the other unit. It is called a reverse channel because the checking data flow is in the opposite direction of the actual data flow.

Half-duplex MODEMs are not used much anymore, but they are still useful and plentiful in some areas of the world.

Full-duplex MODEMs

Similar in functionality to the half-duplex MODEM, full-duplex MODEMs utilize two sets of frequencies, one set that the MODEM transmits on, and one set that it receives on. For example, the Bell 103 type of MODEM uses 1070Hz to transmit a "0" (SPACE) and 1270Hz to transmit a "1" (MARK). It listens for data from the remote MODEM on 2025Hz for a "1" (MARK) and on 2225Hz for a "0" (SPACE). Needless to say, the MODEM on the opposite end has its receive and transmit frequencies reversed. There is no reverse channel on a full-duplex MODEM as none is needed.

MODEM Terminology

There are a few terms associated with MODEMs that the user of such devices should be aware of:

1. Originate Only - this means that the MODEM can only be used for "dial-out" operations; other units dialing the MODEM is not permitted.

2. Answer Only - the MODEM will only answer incoming calls. Outgoing calls cannot be placed.

3. Auto-answer - the MODEM will answer incoming calls.

4. Local and remote diagnostics - this means that the MODEM has the capability of performing manual or automatic self-diagnostics or may be remotely dialed-up for a diagnostic session.

MODEM Standards

It is readily apparent that most MODEM manufacturers in the United States use the AT&T MODEM standards in their designs. As such, a list of the different types of MODEM standards is in order to understand what each one is used for. First, however, here is a breakdown of MODEM speed usages. Remember that MODEM speed is measured in baud (bits per second as allowed by the modulation rate of the signal). Also, baud does NOT translate directly to bits per second (although in many cases it is close). In any electrical transmission, the amount of time allocated to transmit a "1" or a "0" is determined by the architecture of the hardware or by the clocking factor. Baud is the number of signals that can be transmitted in one second. For instance, a signal duration of 20 milliseconds would yield the equivalent of about 50 baud. As you can see, contrary to popular belief, baud is NOT the same as bits per second. Also, remember that the faster the speed, the more the cost.

1. 50, 75 - used in very low speed applications.

2. 110 - used on Teletype Corporation's Model 33 and 35 teleprinters.

3. 134.5 - used on IBM Model 2741 and Model 1050 terminals.

4. 150 - used on Teletype Corporation's Model 37 teleprinter and on other modern terminals using electronic rather than mechanical transmitter/receiver units.

5. 200 - British Post Office DATEL 200 service. Popular in European Post, Telephone and Telegraph (PTT) services.

6. 300 - maximum speed of Bell 103A MODEM and similar full-duplex switched telephone network MODEMs. Also very popular with home hobbyist groups as an inexpensive interface to large system networks. Also low speed setting of Bell 212A full-duplex MODEM.

7. 600 - transmit speed on European-standard split speed MODEMs. Not seen often in the U.S., split speed MODEMs are very popular in Europe for their versatility and functionality (600/1200 split speed).

8. 1200 - maximum speed of Bell 202 and similar half-duplex MODEMs. Also maximum speed of Bell 212A full-duplex MODEM. Popular speed in Europe for split speed MODEMs (600/1200, 1200/75, 75/1200).

9. 1800 - maximum speed of Bell 202 and similar half/full-duplex asynchronous MODEMs on private line (leased line) service. Not a common terminal speed, but popular amongst news wire services, such as AP and UPI.

10. 2400, 4800, 9600 - used for terminals on local lines and for communications processor-to-processor. Also popular for public data networks (such as X.25) for trunk multiplexing to host processors. While these MODEMs are typically synchronous, there are newer MODEMs that support 2400 to 9600 baud communications for asynchronous dial-up communications.

11. 19.2K, 56K - high-speed data communications lines for processor-to-processor communications. These speeds are usually seen on leased lines ONLY and are synchronous. It should be very obvious

that when communicating MODEM to MODEM, the MODEM types must be compatible with each other. For instance, communication between a 300 baud MODEM and an 1800 baud MODEM is quite impossible, but two 300 baud MODEMS will communicate nicely. It should also be noted that the same transmission mode must be compatible: full-duplex to full-duplex, half-duplex to half-duplex.

12. T1 (1.544 Mbit) - very high-speed communications lines for pro-cessor-to-processor and communications interface internetwork-ing.With the advent of the Integrated Services Digital Network (ISDN — described later), the use of T1 will increase dramatically in the next few years.

Now that we have seen what speeds are used for what purposes, let's see the AT&T standards that apply to them:

1. 300 baud async - Bell 103J/113A/212A for leased line or for dial-up line. The 103J and 113A are 300 baud full-duplex ONLY, whereas the 212A is a 300/1200 baud (switchable) full-duplex MODEM.

2. 1200 baud async - Bell 202T/212A for leased line and Bell 202S/212A for dial-up lines. The 202 type of MODEM is simplex or half-duplex (202S/T compatible with 202C, 202D with Bell 804, 202E, and 202R without reverse channel), where the 212A is simplex, half-duplex, or full-duplex (compatible with most 100 series MODEMs in low speed, 212A in high speed).

3. 1200 baud sync - Bell 212A (compatible only with another Bell 212A).

4. 1800 baud - Bell 202T for leased line. Like above, it is still only simplex or half-duplex. This device is nonsynchronous or asyn-chronous (compatible with 202D, 202C, 202E, and 202R without reverse channel).

5. 2400 baud sync - Bell 201C for leased line or network exchange and dial-up. Works at full-duplex and half-duplex (compatible with older 201B and variable speed 209A) and is synchronous only.

6. 4800 baud sync - Bell 208A for leased line and Bell 208B for dial-

up. Works at full-duplex or half-duplex (compatible with variable speed 209A) synchronous only.

7. 9600 baud sync - Bell 209A for leased line or network exchange and for signal multiplexing (TDM). Full-duplex or half-duplex (compatible with 201C and 208A), this MODEM requires D1 or D2 high performance data conditioning. Synchronous only.

8. 19.2K baud sync - Bell 303B for leased line. Synchronous.

9. 56K baud sync - Bell 303C for leased line. Synchronous.

10. T1 - No solid specification yet, but forthcoming

By now you should have a good idea of the types of AT&T MODEMs available and what speeds are generally used for some applications. Be aware that Bell is not the only MODEM company around and that they lease all MODEMs and sell some. Companies that make MODEMs include Anderson-Jacobson, Communications Research Corporation (CRC), Digital Equipment Corporation (DEC), International Business Machines (IBM), Hayes, Racal-Vadic, Paradyne and many others. Purchasing MODEMs is a tricky business and should be carefully considered. At a minimum, always ask yourself the following questions before purchase:

1. Is it compatible with the system/terminal I will be using?

2. Can I get local maintenance? If a large order, can I get on-site maintenance?

3. If communications with Bell MODEMs, is it compatible?

4. Can the company provide me a list of references?

5. What is the Mean Time Between Failures (MTBF)?

6. What is the Mean Time To Repair (MTTR)?

7. If considering split-speed MODEMs (such as 1200/75), is the MODEM FCC and UL compliant (most split-speed MODEMs come from Europe and, as such, may not be FCC and UL compliant)?

8. If considering dual-speed MODEMs (such as the 212A), do I really need both speeds (single speeds are much cheaper)?

9. Do I need full- or half-duplex MODEMs?

10. How big is the physical size of the MODEM (frequently this is a problem that is not discovered until the MODEM is delivered)?

11. Is the MODEM auto-answer, auto-originate, answer-only, or originate-only?

12. Does the selected MODEM meet my needs?

Other Types of MODEMs

There exist on the market a couple of interesting variations of the classical MODEM: the acoustic coupler and the AC MODEM.

Acoustic Couplers

Acoustic couplers are MODEMs with a specially constructed cradle for the hand unit from a standard telephone. The user dials the number of the MODEM attached to the system that the user wishes to use. When the carrier is heard, the handset is placed in the acoustic coupler and the acoustic coupler establishes communications with the host system. This type of MODEM is especially useful for users who have portable terminals or laptop computers or in a situation where multiple users need to use a MODEM in different parts of an organization at various times and modular connectors are not available. Many MODEMs require a four pin or four wire phone jack, usually installed by the phone company. With an acoustic coupler, this is not needed. It should be noted that acoustic are originate-only devices; it's a little tough for the coupler to physically pick up the handset from the phone and stick it in the cradle by itself.

Some companies have taken the acoustic coupler concept and updated it a bit. It is possible to purchase a variation of the acoustic coupler where the acoustic coupler section of the MODEM is reduced to only a device that covers the mouthpiece section of the phone and has an RJ11 jack in it to connect to standard MODEMs. Through this adapter, MODEMs that could previously not be used with certain types of telephones can now be easily used with existing RJ11-connector MODEMs.

AC MODEMs

An increasingly popular device is the AC MODEM. The AC MODEM is a MODEM in the classical sense — it modulates and demodulates a signal — but with a twist: instead of using phone lines or cables to connect local terminals to a system, it uses the AC power lines (wall power sockets). One AC MODEM is connected to the main system and plugged into the wall. The remote MODEM is also plugged into the wall and connected to the remote terminal. Some AC MODEMs, such as Communications Research Corporation's LCM-100, can be located as far away as 800 feet from the host processor and run at speeds up to 9600 baud. This type of MODEM is becoming popular in companies that have a need to rearrange offices on short notice and in companies who leave space and do not wish to install permanent cables to support terminals.

Statistical Multiplexers

Statistical multiplexers, also known as StatMuxes, are used to concentrate multiple communications lines into one line and then to demultiplex the line at the receiving end. StatMuxes are made by a variety of companies (DCA, Timplex, Micom, Digital Equipment Corporation, Dynapac, etc.) and may or may not include integral (built-in) MODEM units. They are usually used in environments where a need to reduce communications costs exists, but custom-developed hardware and software is cost-prohibitive. Let's say that you were the manager of a system in Denver and you had 4 terminals in New York that you wanted to hook up to the system. One method would be to purchase MODEMs for both the system and the terminals and have the terminal users dial-in, but that would be very expensive. Another method might be leased lines for each terminal, but again, that is very expensive. A better solution might be to use a 4-line statistical multiplexer and a 2400 baud leased line between Denver and

New York with the terminals operating at 1200 baud. Some of the benefits to be realized are:

1. The terminals would local to the system, even though they are in New York; no special software to develop and you can use standard interfaces to the system.
2. One phone line to handle all four lines rather than dial-up costs or four leased lines to worry about.

By now you have realized that 1200 x 4 does not equal 2400. On MOST StatMuxes, for a rule of thumb throughput measurement, add up the total aggregate line values (4800) and divide by 2 to get the line value. The lower value is because most statistical multiplexing applications involve terminals; as a result, the terminals are not transmitting at a constant 1200 baud (in this example), thus allowing a lower total line speed. Bear in mind that this is a rule of thumb and you should consult your vendor for actual throughput and load specifications.

StatMuxes come in a variety of configurations and will work on a variety of devices. Most are of the time division multiplex (TDM) type, but there are more and more FDM type multiplexers becoming available on the market. Just like with MODEMs, be aware of the vendor and device before purchase.

Terminal Front-End Processors

Increasingly popular are the varieties of front-end processors (FEP) for mainframes and super mini-computers. A front-end is used to offload terminal "interrupts" (caused by typing a character on a terminal) so that the main processor spends more time doing useful work rather than servicing (taking care of) interrupts. By incorporating front-end processors into system design, a powerful system can usually support more terminals than the system is rated or at least offload input/output (I/O) from terminals, which is a constant problem on all processing systems.

Front-ends are usually true-blue processing systems with terminal interfaces and, most likely, an operating system with special programs. The system then connects to the mainframe or super mini-computer through a local (in the same room) cable. On the host system, depending on the type of front-end used, there may or may not be special software to drive the front-end and service the incoming data from it (the use of special software will depend on the manufacturer of the front-end).

While appealing at first, like with all communications products, be careful in the purchase of front-end processors. Most cost about $1,000.00 per terminal line supported (minimum of 8 lines as a rule), but the cost is coming down as new technological advances are incorporated into front-end design. The front-end should be considered as an integral part of a system and, as such, needs to be systematically analyzed for usefulness with a mix of computer applications software, projected load requirements, expansibility, etc. Most importantly, make sure that your system can handle one and that the vendor of your system (if you have vendor maintenance) will allow you to install such equipment and still maintain a service contract with the vendor.

Communications Front-End Processors

Along the same lines as the terminal front-end processor is the communications front-end processor. As with the terminal FEP, a communications FEP is a fully functional computer system, usually with its own operating system and access method. The difference is that a communications FEP is used to off-load communications computations and protocol overhead. On some systems this can mean significant increases of system throughput.

Communications FEPs come in a variety of configurations and styles, some pre-programmed and some not. Of the preprogrammed variety, most are set up to work with a particular popular protocol or networking architecture. For instance, if TCP/IP were being used, a communications FEP supporting TCP/IP might be useful in offloading the communications processing overhead associated with the network and protocol handling. It is important to remember, however, that the network technology being used must be compatible with the FEPs capabilities or it will not work at all.

Programmable communications FEPs can be very useful in environments where custom programming and support help is available. Many companies use programmable FEPs to provide custom communications processing for items such as automatic teller machines, internal network switching and many other purposes.

Chapter Four

Network Design, Analysis, & Politics

INTRODUCTION

Picking the right network for the job can be a real experience — usually the nauseating type. Selecting a network is the result of a great deal of thought, effort, politics, and general sweat. It can be a very rewarding experience when done correctly or it can be a constant nightmare when done incorrectly. In this chapter we will examine what is involved in network design, things to consider in the design process, the politics of networking, and what constitutes good network design.

What Is Network Design and Analysis?

Network design and analysis is a term networking types apply to the basic methods necessary to PROPERLY design a network. A properly generated network design can provide a company with the following benefits:

o Proper analysis of existing equipment for network installation
o List of requirements for network installation
o Proper configuration of network components for optimum cost savings
o A network topology that is flexible and adaptable
o Correct selection of network hardware for the network function
o Correct selection of network software for the network function
o Documentation of the network for future enhancements and modifications
o Migration path into future network technologies without redesign
o A long network life-cycle (reducing the costs of potential replacement)
o Interconnect paths and methods for multiple network architectures

53

o User analysis and configuration of network resources for optimal use
o Network management plan and methodology to reduce downtime and allow for maximum use of available resources
o Expectations for performance, reliability, and usability
o Optimal programming environment for network(ed) applications
o Training needs for programmers, users, and network managers
o Recurring expense forecasting and budgeting methods
o Network support needs (programming, management, user support)
o Use of mathematical modeling tools to help insure the success of the network design and topology
o Optimal design to prevent network congestion, queuing delay, and proper placement of routing and management resources on the network

Network design is much more than ordering the parts and pieces from a vendor. It is much more than the suggestions the vendor gives you for configuration of your network. As a potential user of network components, you have the final decision on any network configuration and, no matter what the vendor tells you to buy, the final decision to buy rests upon your shoulders. What that means, folks, is that if the network doesn't work as promoted to management, you can blame the vendor, but the ultimate person responsible is you, the person who recommended to management the network components to buy. And, if you think for one second that the smiling vendor across the desk from you is going to recommend some other vendor than himself for your network, you are either naive or you have been listening to too much vendor hype ("We're not here to make money — we're here to be your friend!"). So, remember, the person that will catch the blame from your company in the end is not the vendor — it's you! So, if you want to trust your vendor, great. Personally, there are few people I would consider qualified network designers and you can bet that you are not going to get access to them from a vendor for free. Remember, you get what you pay for.

Identifying the Need

The first step of network design is identification of the need for a network. While this may seem obvious, few companies sit down and spend some time logically defining the reasons for installing a network. Going through this exercise tells you whether or not a network is necessary to accomplish the desired function or whether there is a more cost-effective method to solve the problem at hand. I was asked to design a network for a large financial company one time and, after looking over the needs very carefully, I told them that they didn't need a network. At first, the management of the company thought that I was nuts because their vendor had been hammering on them for months that they needed a network. They simply took it for gospel that they needed one and eventually the vendor got to the upper management and convinced them that they needed a network to solve their "problems." I was called in because the customer didn't know anything about networking and did not have the ultimate confidence in the vendor's efforts to find the "right" solution, regardless of what the vendor solutions were. After working on the project for three weeks, I found that the methodology adopted by the company's management for distributing workload and the reporting hierarchy involved was functioning very well and there was less than 5% out-flow of work to other company entities. What this meant was that 95% of the work being done in the respective branches stayed within the branch and did not require corporate intervention to get work accomplished. Also, all work was done in a reasonable manner and placing a computer in the middle of the paperwork effort would do nothing but slow things down (yes, Virginia, computers are not always better). I went back to the customer's management and explained all of this to them and they immediately called the vendor and demanded an explanation. The vendor told them I was wrong and proceeded to do the one thing that a vendor should never do — cut down the competition. Since I was their "competition," it was obvious to them that I was trying to deprive them of a sale and they felt that they were right and I was wrong. Now I was mad! I spent another two weeks (at the customer's request) thoroughly documenting the lack of need for the network and also fighting some of the irrational claims of the vendor (I asked the vendor once why it was that they were pushing the network so hard when the customer didn't need it; their answer was "Because."). At the end, the vendor backed off their claims as the vendor had not done a thorough (or even partial) job of looking at the customer's needs and how the customer conducted business. The vendor had no idea as to what the customer's plans were for the next fiscal year nor did the vendor bother to look into the budgetary constraints that the customer was under. All the vendor cared about was making the sale — no matter how much the customer did not need it or how much it cost.

The entire hassle could have been avoided if the customer had thought, carefully, about why they "needed" a network. Instead, the customer was heavily influenced by the vendor's sales tactics and got swept up in the buying frenzy that usually accompanies a great many sales of networks. Also, the customer should have looked first to the company business plan — it will tell you whether a network is necessary to achieve the business goals of the company or not, based upon expected market penetration, growth factors, profitability requirements, and personnel requirements. So, rule number one is make sure that you need a network — don't go out and buy one due to unjustified internal pressure, vendor pressure, or peer pressure (yes, we all wish that we had a network just like company X down the street).

What Is a Network Supposed to Do? How Much Is It Going to Cost?

After a need for a network has been established, rule number two in network design is applied: what is it supposed to do and how much is it going to cost?

What it is supposed to do is a matter of defining, very carefully, what functionality the network is to offer. If it is electronic mail, file transfer, or task-to-task communications, great, but WRITE IT DOWN! Also, keep the base functionality of the network clear, concise, and simple. Too many good intentions get shot down because the base rationale was too complex for technical personnel to understand, much less the management personnel who have to approve and budget for it. Remember that your company's management is the signing authority for technical purchases and direction, regardless of what you have been told. If they can't understand what the needs are, you can bet that they will be more than a little apprehensive about installing technology they do not understand. I once told a company that a network does nothing and then explained that if it did anything at all, they should be glad. Setting expectations is very important, and this is accomplished by carefully defining the network functionality.

So far, identification of need and identification of functionality have been defined. Now comes the problem of cost. Networks are just like systems in many ways: they have a life-cycle, they require periodic upgrading and expansion, there are recurring costs such as software and hardware maintenance, telco service, packet services, modems, etc., they require personnel to management and maintain the network components, software may need to be developed so there may be costs for software engineering or applications programming, etc. The point is this: if you think that because network components are less expensive than a given system, think again. The overall cost of services and expansion will show that over a period of time, the network may turn out to be the most costly portion of your overall computing plan. Why? Simple. Networks, for all the high-tech bruhaha they have generated, are very expensive to install and operate over a period of time because they are "service-intensive." What this refers to is the fact that networks require the use of vendor services more than a typical computer system might due to their inherent complexity and lack of a wide understanding of network technology by users, programmers, and managers. Networks are used for communications and communications services are expensive. Yes, networks can save a company a lot of money, IF THEY ARE USED CONSISTENTLY AND PROPERLY. The sad thing is that without proper design, neither consistency or proper use of a network is achieved by most network users. To illustrate how expenses can creep up on you, here are some things that affect the cost of networking:

o Cost of hardware components (modems, cabling, channel interfaces controllers, cabinetry, protocol converters, line conditioners, protocol analyzers, time domain reflectometers, frequency spectrum analyzers, breakout boxes, bit error rate testers, multiplexers, packet assembler/

disassembler boxes, traffic analyzers, response time analyzers, phoneset tester, line testers, manual and automatic switching units, autodialers, protocol simulators, converters, data encryption equipment, auto callback units, data compression units, junction panels, line drivers, protocol converters, repeaters, bridges, voice frequency testers, front-end processors, servers, and many others)

o Cost of software components (networking architecture packages (such as DECnet, SNA, TCP/IP, and others), protocol emulators, protocol conversion, data compression, data analysis, network management, network troubleshooting, network statistics, network security, network applications (such as electronic mail, distributed database applications, office systems, etc.), operating system interfacing software, etc.)

o Cost of operational services (leased-line cost, building conduit space costs, packet-switched network hookups, packet-switched network kilopacket charges, equipment leases, cable installation and add-ons, earth station channel charges, transponder channel charges, dial-up charges (digital service), dial-up charges (analog service), service surcharges for exceeding preagreed usage levels of shared services, general equipment maintenance, software maintenance, pickup/delivery and destination charges, line conditioning, per-call maintenance, per-call consulting services, administrative charges, etc.)

o Cost of consulting (network design, data collection, data reduction and analysis, network topology, traffic matrix, routing matrix, performance models, applications design, applications programming, queueing delay analysis, network technology assessment, network implementation, network installation, network management, network user training, network programmer training, network manager training, network project management, network troubleshooting and fault finding, network enhancements and add-ons, network interconnect design and implementation, interconnect training, network planning, network facilities survey, and many more) o Cost of replacement due to improper initial design (all of the above plus the original cost to implement the current network)

While this may look like an extensive list, it isn't. That means that there are plenty of other costs that can come out of nowhere that were not expected or not properly planned for. You may look at this list and say to yourself that you don't need all the stuff listed above. This may be true, but I feel that with the influx of network technology and the price of the hardware dropping, you will find yourself involved in networking in the near future if you are not already involved. This also means that although you may not use some of the equipment and components listed above, what's to say that you will not later on in your current company or in some other computing life?

Rule Number Three: The Site Survey

The site survey is not a trivial thing. Site surveys involve the careful examination of company facilities, building architecture, phone facilities (if you are using phone lines), existing computer hardware and software components, examination of existing contracts (to see if some already cover the needs for the network), power facilities, HVAC facilities, wireways and wire centers, electromagnetic interference possibilities, radio frequency interference possibilities, safety issues, security issues, building wiring and fire codes, electrical codes, reception and shipping facilities, building maintenance capabilities, on-site or vendor maintenance capabilities, and other related items. While this may initially seem to be not necessary, consider what happened to a friend of mine when he was designing the cable layout for a large electric company. He carefully measured the cable length needs and used a building diagram given to him by the customer as the basis for layout of the wire plan. What he did not know was that he was using an old plan and that many of the walls and wireways had changed. As a result, he planned wire runs directly through the company kitchen, which was not on the building diagram. Fortunately, since a proper site survey involves the customer, software, hardware, sales, service, and other selected personnel, the mis-layout of the wire plan was caught before the plan was finalized and corrections were made. Site surveys involve many people and require quite a bit of time to properly lay out the network in the environment in which it will function and to insure that all the "players" are where they are supposed to be when they are supposed to be there to insure a smooth installation of the network.

Basic Design, Data Collection/Reduction, and Data Analysis

Rule number four is the basic network design, data collection/reduction, and data analysis. Network design, as I said before, is not as simple as throwing the wire down, hooking it up, and tossing some software on the machine. Network design is a science that has grown quite complicated as more and more sophisticated networks have evolved. A network designer starts out by actively and aggressively investigating all the needs, wants, hopes, and aspirations for the network that a company wishes to implement. He then takes the justifications that a company has written up, the functionality statement, and the site survey and identifies missing parts and pieces necessary to the network design. Following collection of data to satisfy the parts and pieces that are missing, the designer sets out to investigate the proper type of technology that the company requires now and to achieve their future goals for the network. Isolation of the proper technology is a critical step in solid network design. By providing alternative technologies, the network designer can give the customer a few good options by which to implement the network, which can result in time and cost savings as well as reducing the risk of a single network technology causing network failures due to flaws, bugs, or other problems. Once a series of technologies has been defined, the designer then uses mathematical modeling tools (manual and computer-based) to figure out data flow ratios, probabilities of error, queueing delays, interconnect problems, least-cost network topological layout, routing paths, redundancy paths, and many more necessary items essential to solid network design. The modeled data is collected and reduced to meaningful facts and figures about the design and compared to network requirements dictated by the customer. If the results fit the requirements window, the network design being analyzed may be useful in the customer's environment (provided it meets physical needs, support needs, etc.). This process is repeated for every reasonable network technology until all the potential technologies are completely modeled. Following the modeling of network data, a financial analysis is done to determine how much the network is going to cost to implement, startup, maintain, and expand. This is another exhaustive analysis that requires thought on the future of the network as well as applying practical experience with the theoretical network model. Finally, an assessment analysis is performed to identify networks that are "most" useful (closest to the desired functionality) and "least" useful (on the right track, but not closest to the desired combination of price/performance/ease of use, etc.). Once all of these items have been done, the network designer takes the results back to the site survey team and works with them to iron out any particular problems with the network designs as well as help isolate which design best suits the needs of the customer.

Another document the network designer will typically generate is one defining personnel needs and operational considerations. This document typically describes the type of personnel necessary to get the job done and what kind of personnel will be necessary for the day-to-day support of the network and its related components. In addition to the base personnel needs, a breakdown of costing for such personnel might also be included.

Once a particular network design has been identified by the network designer and the site survey team, a formal design document is drafted that documents the rationale for the design, a description of the components, a network topology, a wiring diagram, expansion capabilities, expected lifecycle, applications support environment (and package descriptions, if applicable), network management environment, potential problems, data throughput analysis, testing and verification procedures, identification of network installation resources, an implementation timetable, personnel and training needs, cost analysis, and risks. The formal design document is the backbone to the network design and serves as a guideline for implementation and expansion. Following generation of the design document, a presentation is also created for the customer's management so that all parties involved thoroughly understand what the network looks like, what it is capable of doing, what resources are required, how long it will take to implement it and how much it will cost to implement, support, and maintain.

By now you have probably realized that there is not a network in place, yet, and still there have been quite a few people involved and an obvious amount of work has been done. Why go through all this grief just for a network?

The answer is simple and yet complex (the yin and yang of networks): proper business procedure and reduction of potential risks. I had a management friend of mine come up to me once and asked me why all of this was necessary for the sake of installing a wire, some controllers, and some software. I told him that it is like playing the stock market. There are people who buy a stock because it "looks" good; they may not have qualified the prospect, but they have a good feeling about it, so they buy the stock. This is the "gut feel" approach. Sometimes it works, sometimes it doesn't, but studies have proven that it does not work more often than not (about 78% failures). Granted, there are some that seem to know how to use the gut feel approach very well and are very good at it, but these people are few and far between. The second type try to play the stock market on their own. They read up on it for a while, read some analysis work on given stock types, and proceed to use a discount broker to invest their money in stocks that they select. This approach is usually not successful for a very long time due to the long learning curve necessary to play the stock game and the need to watch stocks over a pretty fair piece of time. The self-broker stock player is usually dismally profitable at first and may improve later on if he does not get frustrated and quit first. The third type of stock player is the high-risk options player. This type can be a gambler type and can make a killing or go bust in a matter of a day. Options players have to really understand the market to play well and profit. The fourth type is the stock player that uses a broker to invest his money in stocks in hopes that the broker can pick the right stocks and make the right decisions to generate a profit for the stock player. This is somewhat akin to using a consultant: there are very, very good stock brokers, but there are a lot of mediocre or poor stock brokers who are not overly cautious with their customer's investments and can ruin potentially reasonable deals. The final type of stock player is one who is a stock expert and can play the game himself with confidence due to his in-depth and expert understanding of the stock market. I then told my friend that most people are very leery about playing the stocks by themselves. I asked him how many options players he knew and how many expert stock players he knew. He answered that he didn't know any. Most people interested in the stock market try to find a good broker and the amount they pay the broker is worth it for the lower risk they are taking, the lack of need to become a "guru" in the stock market methodology, not to mention the reduction in time that it takes to monitor their investment.

When looking at network design and analysis, the main mistake that many companies make is that they approach a network in the same manner that they might approach the self-broker methodology. Nothing could be worse. Networks have some fairly serious restrictions on them that many systems do not, as well as the fact that there are many more systems "experts" than there are network "experts" due to the complexity of network design as well as the lack of general network design education, and information. Most systems have training and documents available for learning the hows and whys of systems hardware and software. Networks, unfortunately, are subject to the whims of multiple types of systems trying to talk to one another, frequently on differing technology, and take on dimensions that most systems never have to worry about. Compound that with a severe lack of good, clear user documentation, technology information, and design documentation. Network designers capable of designing superior networks are few and far between and usually rely on heavy experience and learning networking "the hard way."

If you have been scared to death about network design and analysis as a result of reading the previous paragraphs, good! It also means that you may now realize that the proper design of a network is critical to making the network cost-effective over the long run as well as understanding that just because you have sharp systems people, they may not be able to design a network properly due to lack of information and experience. Using consultants in the network design phase can help drastically reduce the risk factor of the network, and a good consultant can tell you what he can do and what you can do. This will save money in the short and long term, as well as provide you a solid network design. While it is true that you can design your network yourself, it is not necessarily true that the network will survive over the long haul nor can you feel comfortable that it will perform as expected if you have not done a performance analysis before the network is in place. Proper network design can save a ton of money down the road and is cost-effective up-front if done correctly. If you are penny-wise and dollar-foolish, you will, indeed, end up paying later.

Networking Politics

In my earlier days of technical absorbence, I spent most of my time worrying about whether I was doing the right technical "thing" or not. Many times I would spend many hours contemplating the ultimate protocol or the ideal network application. This, of course, would many times fall on deaf management ears, which is something I found very hard to understand. Why was it that management rarely paid attention to my grandiose ideas and lofty thoughts? Worse yet, why was it that it seemed that I was constantly avoiding corporate politics?

Technical people tend to sneer loudly and longly at corporate politics. It would be nice if there were none, but companies seem to thrive on politics, so ignoring them does nothing but compound the problem of dealing with politics. In the networked environment, however, politics take on a whole new role.

In my years of networking experience, I have spent many hours explaining the networks I design and implement over and over to corporate management structures. The need for the re-explanation is frequently due to the diversity of corporate management at different locations the network connects to. Fred, for instance, in Denver has a computer room full of processors and communications equipment. John, in Tucson, has a similar set-up. Jeff in L.A., like the good corporate man he is, insists on equal treatment and has a like configuration. Now Charles, the president of the company, sends out an edict that all computers will communicate with each other and that said communication will be in the most efficient method possible. Enter me. My responsibility was to: a) configure a least-cost network, and b) implement same. Sounds good on paper, right? That's about as far as it got for a long time.

When designing and configuring networks, funny things creep in that make no logical sense, have no basis for reasonable reality, and are of questionable use. These things are called politics. Many companies seem to have this implicit checklist: network design, check; documentation, check; politics, double check (got to make sure to get that included, just for excitement). Anyway, this network was no different. Because of a deal the company had set up with a long distance phone carrier, the cheapest phone line route was to connect L.A. to Tucson and Tucson to Denver, utilizing Tucson as a routing point for traffic to/from Denver. From a network configuration point of view, the situation was inexpensive, throughput was reasonable, queueing delay tolerable, and maintainability was reasonable. That, unfortunately, was the easy part. Implementation, well, that turned out to be a different story.

The Real Story

It seems that good 'ole Fred in Denver and John in Tucson are not the best of friends. As a matter of fact, there was very little love lost between the two, and both tended to avoid one another like the plague. As a result, the use of the Tucson facility as the routing point was absolutely unacceptable to good 'ole Fred. Not that the routing was a bad thing or that the financials were bad. No, that wasn't it at all. The problem was that Fred's data was dependent upon John's center routing data to and fro, and Fred did not feel comfortable with that idea. Also, Fred was paranoid enough to feel that John might deliberately try to cause general communications problems that could severely disrupt Fred's ability to do business and look wonderful in the management eye. Such is the nature of politics: an emotional response to a business situation. Fred, intellectually, understands that the best method to set up the network is through Tucson, but he does not like the idea of depending upon John to provide him his data communications reliability. John, on the other hand, understands the kind of hold that he would have over Fred and, as such, was urging that the network be configured and installed as quickly as possible so that it would be configured as drawn up. This way, John would have some control over Fred, further enhancing his position in the company and also control the intercorporate "rival."

What we have just seen is not all that unusual. The more nodes a network has, the better the chance of politics invading the design and operation of the network. This is especially prevalent where there is competition between the various centers networked together and the centers are dependent upon each other for technical support and assistance. Worse yet is when each of the centers are contributing "funds" towards operation of the network and/or systems they use. In that type of environment, each center can develop either prosupport services or antisupport services depending upon the management flavor of each center or the competency (at least the perceived competency) of the support staff. Another problem of the central support with contributed funds issue is the problem of machine ownership. Ultimately, all machines are owned by the corporate. However, since center managers are graded based upon their performance and fiscal prowess, they will get very possessive over the systems and resources they have a day-to-day interest in using. As a result, soon the systems that are "owned" by the corporation are now "owned" by the center and corporate support staff have to get permission to "work on OUR machines." The OUR machine syndrome is caused by upper corporate management not understanding the "who owns what" problem and keeping the ownership and support issues controlled by corporate policy or edict. Center managers then develop turfish attitudes towards "their" systems and network components and can be very difficult to deal with if they are not getting good corporate systems and network support.

Location of Nodes and Politics

Distribution of locations, a common trait of larger networks, increases the political problem of network design and management. Systems design is usually done by someone familiar with local applications or needs (possibly even the local support personnel are involved). Networks, however, have to look at the corporate problem and sometimes the corporate need is outweighed by the individual center's need, much to the chagrin of the individual center. As a result, the networking support types are looked upon with disdain by the maligned center and things go downhill from there. Geographic dispersion also precludes the use of good, solid communications between PEOPLE. Many times, body english, gestures, attitudes, and other traits are easily recognized in a face-to-face that are not recognized in electronic mail or over the phone conversations. It is, therefore, very important to set up a good, solid rapport with the management of each geographical location so that everyone knows each other and a good feeling of support is available across all centers the network touches. Users at all locations will talk to each other and, if one center is being treated like the bastard child, you can bet that the remainder of the users at the other locations will know about it in a short amount of time. Bad news travels fast.

Avoiding network politics will do nothing but increase the political problem as a whole. To help you keep the politics to a minimum, consider the following items for prospective network managers and support personnel:

1. Communications between people is all-important. Always spend a great deal of time describing and documenting for the user base what you are doing and why.
2. Always get the local management at each location involved. Noninvolvement will increase the local paranoia (which is always there).
3. Don't underestimate any user on the network. Keep all users content, where possible and reasonable.

4. Good rapport is all-important when dealing with various locations. Get to know the users and management at all locations and keep everyone in the loop. They WILL talk to each other, so don't be surprised to find out that an offhand comment in Denver ends up being an ISSUE in L.A.
5. Taking an attitude of "I'm technical and don't do politics" will do nothing but increase your political problems. In the networked environment, politics are part of the design and support, so get used to it.
6. If possible, get some sensitization training. There is nothing worse to a user than a surly answer from the support organization. Always be empathetic for the user, but keep the sympathy to a minimum.
7. If you do not write well, get some training. If your secretary writes well (many are very good), let him or her clean up any corporate communications you issue. Written communication is very important to tracing problems in the political structure.
8. If a political situation arises, take ACTION but, under no circumstances, REACT to the situation. Many political moves happen due to power plays, inconsideration, or just to stir things up. If one arises, never let your emotions get in the way of solid, logical reasoning and fact. It's real easy to get caught up in the flurry of politics if one is not very careful. Be ever watchful, however, to identify a political problem from a real problem. If there is a system down, that's a real problem and don't escalate it into a political one.

What Makes Good Network Design?

What we have discussed so far are the generalities of the network design process and the politics of networking. With that information dutifully digested, what constitutes a good network design?

Good network design is characterized by the following main points:

1. It meets or exceeds the needs defined in the specification
2. It is cost effective and cost predictable
3. Its capabilities are obvious and beneficial

4. It is capable of being managed by system-manager level personnel
5. It is user-friendly, or, preferably, user-transparent
6. It is easily expanded
7. It is well documented
8. The technology is state of the practice, not state of the art
9. It is supportable and maintainable at all node locations
10. Network diagnostics and management are thought out and available
11. The network provides for future interconnectivity
12. The network has predictable performance as loading changes
13. Its load on networked systems is predictable and reasonable
14. It provides security adequate to the corporate or applications needs
15. It is upgradable as systems are upgraded and enhanced
16. It survives the politics of the company and provides for political needs

There is no reason that a network should not provide for all the above list. Proper network design will generate a network topology and architecture that will provide for all the above topics.

While some of the above list is quite obvious, there are some items that should be explained in a bit more detail.

Cost Effective and Cost Predictable

Cost effective is fairly obvious. The network components obviously have to justify their economic existence, or a company is simply wasting money. Cost predictable, however, is different. Over the period of life of any network, there is a need to predict the costs the network will incur upon corporate financials. Some of the more obvious costs include component upgrades, software maintenance, hardware maintenance, and operational management tools and personnel. Some of the less obvious costs that need to be predictable are documentation, training, code maintenance, system downtime due to network component failure, productivity delays due to congestion or failure of the network, consulting assistance, and other obscure costs. When the network is designed, such costing needs to be planned carefully so that no surprises surface after the fact.

Obvious Capabilities and Benefits

The network must have obvious capabilities and it must be able to demonstrate those capabilities upon demand. This is necessary due to the recognition by management of the merits and necessity of the network and its capabilities. Once management recognition is attained, the needs of the network can be addressed properly and funding for the network assured. It is also important that management understand not only where the network fits into the scheme of things, but also what the network means to corporate resources, management, and productivity so that a total picture is possible. If the network is obviously useful and beneficial, the life of the network can be more easily justified, and the corporation will utilize the network and its capabilities in all appropriate areas.

Capable of Being Managed by Systems-Management Personnel

A network that is so complex that it cannot be managed by in-place systems management personnel is too complex to be used in a day-to-day operational environment. We would all like to think that we have systems gurus on staff that can handle anything, but such is not the case. And, unless the network manager on staff has ownership of the company (and even then in some cases), chances are very good that he/she will seek greener pastures someday, leaving the company with some serious network problems if the network is unmanageable.

Expansion

A network should be able to be expanded without redesigning the entire network. It is also very important to note that if the network has not been designed to be expandable, it is doomed to failure almost from the inception. I recently had a customer ask me to do a base network design for some PCs that they were putting into place for access to their super-minicomputer. I started running through my standard list of required items to consider when I asked them how many systems they were going to network together. Their answer?

"Eight to ten. There shouldn't be any others."

After I finished laughing, they asked me why I was laughing. It was very simple. In over 80% of the networks I have designed in the last 10 years, those 80% have always expanded by 100% in the first year of operation due to productivity enhancements given by the network, better work environment, and political pressure to "be tied into the network." And you know something? I was right. It has now been about two years and the network has expanded from 10 original PCs and 2 superminis to 6 super-minis and over 50 PCs (they exceeded the 100% growth figure the first year). Fortunately, I had designed the network to handle the growth, and it will continue to grow without problems for a long time to come.

Expansion is very important even if the current management is claiming no expansion. Management structures change, corporate directions change, people change. There is no reason that the network should not be able to do so as well.

The Network Is Well Documented

Proper documentation of how the network was configured, why, and the politics behind it is critical to future support, expansion, and interpretation of the original goals of the network. How many times have you run into a situation where something was in place that was a piece of junk and you could not find out why it was done the way it was? So, you correct it into your own image and likeness and the guy from Casper, Wyoming, who uses the system once a quarter, gets three kinds of upset because you changed it and he was promised that it would not be changed and it was put on paper that way. Without proper documentation, you can get called all kinds of names after the fact because no one may understand the hows and whys of the network. It is critical for proper management, support, and expansion that the network be thoroughly and carefully documented.

State of the Practice, Not State of the Art

State of the practice means that the network architecture reflects proven, useful, current technology that is not leading edge. Why not leading edge, you say? I'm glad you asked.

Leading edge technology is good for the daredevils, but it has no place in the business or engineering environment unless it is the only reasonable method to get the job done. This is because of support, expansion, and technology acceptance problems. More specifically, leading edge technology usually has a ton of bugs and problems, there are few people who understand it (and they are very expensive), it imposes unnecessary risk upon the functionality of the network (new technology is always very risky), and it may not receive wide acceptance upon review by the industry and other vendors.

State of the practice technology reflects that which is used. It may not be the latest thing on the market, but it is proven, reliable, manageable, cost predictable, and talent to manage the technology is available. State of the practice technology is also easier to sell to management, as successful installations in the same industry grouping as your own can usually be found and the risk to corporate cash and business is greatly reduced, two main factors in management blessing of network components and capabilities.

When working with and configuring networks, it is essential that cost and risk constantly be kept in mind. If these issues can be addressed with a functional, cost-effective network solution, the network and the corporation will be successful in their network endeavors for some time to come.

Interconnectivity

Few companies configure networks for one type of computer. Whether the main vendor in-house is IBM, DEC, CDC, or any other is irrelevant, as all major (and minor) computer vendors usually offer a variety of computer models, architectures, and technologies. As a result, computer networks must provide for interconnectivity of existing architectures and future architectures that emerge as a result of network and corporate expansion. So, even if all your shop bleeds is IBM blue, remember that getting the PCs to connect to the 3083 may be a real pain and you need to plan ahead for the eventuality.

Predictable Performance as Loading Changes

Systems performance will change over the life of any system. This is due to the inability of users and systems managers to properly utilize available systems components when the system is initially configured (and the system is underutilized) to the level where all the users are knowledgeable and beat the hell out of the system at all times of the day or night. Both situations cause problems in network design. In the first instance, the network works fine or, if the network has inherent performance problems, it provides marginal performance. In the second instance, the system suffers, the network components suffer, and the entire network can suffer as well if the system is in a critical path within the network.

Consider this. Let's suppose that the node we are interested in is a routing node for an entire group of nodes. At first, the node is lightly loaded and is doing a good job of routing traffic from system to system. Later on, however, the necessity for running additional jobs becomes apparent and the systems group gets the management edict to use whatever resources are available to get the job done. As a result, the lightly used routing node now becomes heavily used. The network routing software now has to contend for CPU time with jobs running on the system, and the data being routed through the loaded node becomes more and more delayed. As a result, nodes that were expecting the data to arrive experience delays and the entire group of nodes slows down and cannot get the same amount of work done. The end result? Throughput is drastically reduced on all nodes in the group, and the networks and systems suffer as a result (not to mention the productivity loss of the users and other such horrible things).

When considering network performance, it is necessary to look at not only the network topology and components, but also the loading history of critical processor and applications to insure that there is a clear picture as to how fast things are going to perform and how well.

Security Is Adequate for Corporate and Network Needs

Security is an elusive thing. First off, I'm going to hack off a lot of people by saying that networks are not secure. I mean it! I have proven time and again that a network can be broken into by any node on the network. While it is quite possible to make it very difficult to break into a network, it is similar to car theft: you can't keep out professionals. If they want into your network bad enough, there is very little you can do to stop them.

Most knowledgeable security and audit personnel know this, and it is part of the risk vs. cost decisions that are made by upper management. A network should strive for a totally secure environment, but such an environment should allow for cost-intelligent placement of security vs. how much management wants to spend to keep the network and related systems secure. Also, as a rule, people with network access (and especially if they have systems privileges on any given node) can usually get at the network in a short amount of time and target a node where the security is weak. Through this method of attack, hostile users can access, slowly but surely, most of the nodes that they wish to access and in a manner that is extremely difficult if not impossible to trace.

To insure the success of the network, a security audit should be done during the design phase to know where the network and its components are vulnerable and what can be gained through a penetration. This information can then be made available to management and a management decision rendered as to how much needs to be spent to clear up any deficiencies that management feels are critical to the security of the corporation.

Upgradability as Systems and the Network Are Enhanced

As you are aware, it is impractical to expect the network software and hardware to be upgraded simultaneously within all systems as new software and hardware become available. Not only is this a difficult logistical problem, the practicalities are quite difficult as well. Unless there is a small number of small processors that are lightly used, any systems upgrade, as a rule, will disrupt operations on any given machine, and any given machine may potentially disrupt operations on an entire network if the upgrades are not carefully considered networkwide.

A good network design will allow for network and systems upgrades and provide for a method to do both. Solid network design requires that the future be considered as well as the present.

Survivability of Company Politics and Political Needs

Network designs must encompass not only the needs of the technical end, but also the needs of the practical end. The practical end encompasses the day-to-day needs of the corporation as well as the political needs of its management. If the network does nothing but disrupt the political alignment of the company, there will be nothing but resentment and problems that come with it, as well as blame and search for a scapegoat upon which to heap the wrath.

For a network to survive the political environment, care must be taken to allow proper placement of the network in the political environment. If the network is not properly introduced, placed, and controlled by the appropriate level of management, the political machine can turn on the network and associated personnel and proceed to squash everything in its path.

Chapter Five

Network Architecture

INTRODUCTION

When the topic of networking comes up, one of the first things that gets mentioned is network architecture. It's a great buzzword; it sounds very official, impresses management, and is a good thing to say when mentioning networks. Besides, when networking, do as the networkers do.

What Is Network Architecture?

Network architecture is a fancy term for the way that networking products are constructed. Networking hardware and software is implemented on systems via a mechanism called network or communications architecture. Communications architecture is the "layering" of software based upon the functionality of each layer. It is very similar to an organization chart at a corporation. At the lowest level of the protocol layers lies the data link access, the software used to talk directly to the hardware. This is usually a cryptic interface and is difficult to implement and maintain. At the next level would be some sort of communications line handler whose job would be to keep messages sorted out and manage connection creation and destruction between machines. The next layer up would be a session control mechanism responsible for the overall message flow control and ensuring that the communication "session" between systems goes smoothly. The remainder of the upward layers is dedicated to direct user program interaction for specific functions. For example, one layer would be used for communications with programs desiring remote file access and manipulation, another with program-to-program communications, etc. Very few communications architectures do not use layered architectures, and those that do not use layered architectures are somewhat antiquated. The

77

benefits of the layered approach are many, but the most significant one is the ability to change a layer's capabilities without significantly modifying the entire architecture. This feature alone makes a layered network architecture very attractive for companies desiring inter and intra systems communications capability.

What Started All the Rush?

There was a time when there was no such thing as a network architecture. Companies implemented rather rude, crude, and socially unacceptable software and hardware communications solutions without any thought as to layering or to the implementation of an architecture. The idea of layering really took off with the introduction of an international standard called the Open Systems Interconnect (OSI) model by the International Organization for Standardization (ISO) in 1982 (International Standard 7498).

In 1978, the ISO Technical Committee 97 (they're the folks that handle standardization of information technology) started subcommittee number 16 (TC97/SC16) to develop an architecture and reference model that would serve as the foundation for future standards activities. From 1978 onwards, they have worked very hard at providing a flexible, reasonable communications architecture that could be implemented on a variety of systems and provide inter and intra systems communications capabilities in a variety of environments. Oddly enough, TC97/SC16 has not done most of the work on defining the protocols for each layer of the architecture; other ISO committees have done this, using the model specified by TC97/SC16. Even at this writing, all protocols for all layers have not been defined yet, but the model still is highly useful in the definition of how a communications architecture is defined.

What Do the Layers Do?

To understand the OSI a little better, let's examine what each layer does.

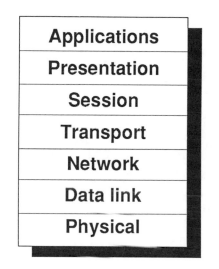

The Open Systems Interconnect (OSI) Model

Above a diagram of the OSI model is given. You will notice that the model is basically seven tiers, stacked one upon the other, that reflects a certain function at each layer. User data comes in to the top layer (layer seven) and travels through the various layers of protocols until it finally goes out over the transmission medium (hardware). It then travels to the destination node and begins its travel up the layers of protocols on the remote system until it reaches the destination program on the remote system. This same ordeal happens on all communicating systems for the duration of communications between nodes.

The following few paragraphs define the functionality of each layer of the OSI model:

Layer 1 - Physical Layer

This is the touch-and-feel layer. The Physical layer provides for the transparent transmission of bit streams from one physical entity to another (or many, as in the case of datagram oriented services such as Ethernet).

Layer 2 - Data Link Layer

The Data Link layer handles the transfer of data between the ends of a physical link.

Layer 3 - Network Layer

The Network layer handles the routing and switching of information to establish a connection for the transparent delivery of data.

Layer 4 - Transport Layer

The Transport layer provides for error-free delivery of data and also acts as the control area for quality of service requirements for the selected data service.

Layer 5 - Session Layer

Session layer provides the coordination between communicating processes between nodes ("virtual" connectivity).

Layer 6 - Presentation Layer

The Presentation layer provides for any format, translation, or code conversion necessary to put the data into an intelligible format.

Layer 7 - Applications Layer

The Applications layer allows the end application to communicate with the communications architecture by providing the appropriate communications service(s) to the application.

At each layer, there may be one or more protocols (in the case of layer 2 and above) or communications media (in the case of layer 1) that communicates with a peer protocol or media on the complementary node (s). What this means is that, at any level, there can be more than one way to get data to and from the node; the only requirement is that there be the same peer at the destination node that understands what is sent.

At first this may all seem a bit chaotic and it is — to an extent. It is the job of the communications architect and software/hardware engineers to put the right functionality in the right spots to keep throughput of the network high and the overhead of sending data back and forth low. If you consider each layer to have its own protocol, or filter, it is somewhat easier to understand. I tend to look at communications architectures like a glorified air purifier system. One program takes a packet of pure air and starts sending it to another program on a remote node. To insure its purity, each layer of the communications architecture puts a special container around the pure packet of air so that it will not get contaminated on the way. This means that by the time the packet of pure air is out the node, it basically has 6 containers around it (when it is traveling, it is in container 1, the physical layer). When the packet reaches its destination, it travels up the layers, with each protocol removing the container that it knows how to remove, inspecting for damage, and, if no damage is present, sending it up to the next layer. If a layer finds damage, the packet is thrown away (it's contaminated) and the source node is requested to send another pure packet of air (we can't have bad air getting to our pure air environment). This is the typical path that most data takes when using communications architectures and the layered approach.

To compound misery, communications architectures do much more than send data. Nodes (systems) need to know which nodes are available for access, which services (layers) are active, and, in some nodes, if routing is necessary. To do this, many communications architectures keep a database of active nodes, known nodes (nodes the system knows about but that may not necessarily be up and running or available), and nodes that are down. Still more, some systems on a network are known as routing nodes.

A Routing Node Is a Tired Node

End Node   **End Node**

Routing Node

Three Nodes with B Being the Router

A routing node basically is a node that is very smart as to the topology of the network and how to talk to other nodes. A routing node is nothing more than a relay point. It is not magical, mystical, or hard to understand. Let's suppose that we need to go from node A to node C, but the only way to get there is through node B. In this example, A cannot "see" C, but B can. C cannot "see" A, but B can. So, since B "sees" both A and C, it is logical to presume that B can get the data from A to C. If B were a routing node, this would be possible. The packet of pure air would leave node A, travel up the architecture on node B until it hit the proper layer that handles routing functions (the NETWORK layer), upon which the layer would strip off its container and find that the packet does not belong on its node, but, instead, belongs on node C. Node B would then put a new container around the packet specifying node C as the destination and send the packet on its merry way. C would receive the packet and it would travel up C's protocol layers until it got to the destination program. See how simple it is? It's like leaving a message at the answering service. You call the service, leave a message, and hang up. The service calls the destination (either immediately or, in some cases of store and forward, later) and delivers the message from you to the destination. Piece of cake!

Some types of communications architectures employ different schemes to implement routing capability, but the basic concept is usually the same: you send it to the routing node and it passes it on to the appropriate destination. On some networks, there may be many, many routing nodes to pass packets back and forth between destinations. In those cases, a routing node may not have direct access to the destination, but it would know which routing node would have direct access and would send the data to the next routing node in the line to get to the destination node until the data finally reached its destination. If, for some reason, there was a breakdown in communications somewhere along the path, the initiating node would be informed of the break and allowed to re-transmit the packet or the communications path (link) would be destroyed (broken).

When considering communications on a network architecture, there is a lot more going on than immediately meets the eye. Consider the system performing routing functions for nodes on a network. That system may not have had much of a load on it before the network. Now that the network software has been installed and activated, the node will have work to do even if no data is being transmitted. When nodes are idle, they will usually send HELLO and TEST messages to each other. It's like being Maytag repairmen — they get lonely, so they need to communicate periodically to make sure that they are all still healthy and active. If the node being considered is a routing node, it can get beat on pretty hard even though it is not the destination for the data on the network. The "check and forward" operation that a routing node performs can drink up processor resources and cause degradation of the processor. If the processor is not very powerful, it can also degrade the network fairly substantially!

Imagine that everyone had to go to the same butcher in a small community. The butcher is capable of handling the load because he is diligent and has adequate resources to handle his clientele. Ah, but what happens when the new housing subdivision is built? Well, the butcher now gets new business that he did not have before. And, since he is the only butcher in town, he gets a lot of new business and expands his shop to handle his business. At first he can handle the new business by adding newer cutting devices, adding a room, and adding some additional personnel. His reputation grows, the community grows, his business grows. One day, however, the people start complaining about the lack of service, the long waits in line for checkout, and other delays. The butcher now has to make a decision: build a new shop or expand the new one. Well, expanding the old one may be out of the question if there is no room to expand. And building a new shop may be out of the question because of the cost and risk involved with a new shop in unknown territory or with an unstable clientele. So, the butcher can either get more work done more efficiently, expand, or add shops. Such is the quandary of routing as well: expand the routing node resources, add new routing nodes (and split up the work load), or replace the node with a completely new mechanism to handle the increased load.

A routing node is not a butcher shop, but there are many similarities. When packets have to wait to be routed, they are queued or put into a line in a holding place. Later they are dequeued and processed by the routing software and requeued to the next layer down. The time it takes to perform this enqueueing, dequeueing, and reenqueueing is called queueing delay and is the ultimate enemy of any network. You may have the fastest communications hardware in the world. You may have the biggest IBM or DEC processor that is made on each end. But, if the traffic is routed through an IBM PC, expect the traffic to take a while to get to where it is going (for those of you who are laughing, I've seen that happen, so don't judge lest ye be judged).

Delays of the Queueing Type

Queues are everywhere on computer systems and in communications architectures, so learn to live with them. No packet of data goes straight to a device unless the engineering was done within very tight specifications and the network has a very limited usage. Most queueing of data happens in the software and usually involves multiple queues at each layer of the communications architecture. To compound the agony of delay, most operating systems impose additional queues (especially multiuser operating systems), which must be used to get data to and from its destination. The more queues an architecture has, the more the chance for bottlenecks at any given queue or group of queues. Also, the overhead of processing data to and from queues will impact processor performance and, as a result, network throughput.

Now that we understand the basics of routing and queueing delay, what else is necessary to understanding network architecture? Glad you asked (Isn't it amazing how you seem to ask the right questions at the right time!?).

Physical, Logical, and Error Control

There are three other basic concepts that are necessary to understanding network architecture: physical link control, logical link control, and error handling.

Physical link control usually starts happening in the transport layer of the communications architecture. The idea is to find the right physical line that is associated with the direction that the data needs to go to get to the proper remote destination. If it sounds like transport and network layers talk to each other a lot, they do! The transport layer insures that the containers sent from one node are intact when they reach the destination node. It also worries about a thing called quality of service, which is necessary to insure that the transmission linkage from A to B is good, reliable, and within specified error tolerances. The transport container contains software to provide the ability to multiplex data streams to a destination node (such as the case where multiple programs are accessing the same node on a network — no point in duplicating effort, is there?), establishing the optimum size of data packets for transmission (if the line is good, then packet sizes may be higher; if it is bad, it may need to be smaller), detecting errors in received data, checking for duplicate data packets, taking care of misdelivered packets, expediting delivery for some classes of packets (such as network control packets), and purging data when a link get zapped to expedite recovery of the network and the linkage to the remote system (if applicable).

Logical link control happens at the session layer and is the "virtual" connection between systems. The idea of session control is to allow programs requesting network access the ability to tell the network architecture "Get me to node A" without having to specify the hows and whys. Session control sets up a "session" between the programs on the nodes and feeds information to the lower layers to allow the communications "session" to flow smoothly. Some vendors have set up their lower level protocols to allow multiple hardware connections between the same nodes. In this situation, the session layer would tell transport to connect node A with node B, but not which hardware device to use. If the hardware device should fail in the middle of the "session," transport layer could take action and fail over to the working hardware to the remote node. In this fashion, the "session" is kept intact and the source and destination programs never detect a break in communications at all. Session control would work with transport to make sure that the recovery was transparent to the communicating programs and communication, while slightly delayed due to the recovery, would still go on (which is the idea of a network, nicht wahr?).

Finally, error control. The concept of error control is fairly obvious: controlling and correcting errors that happen. If anyone tells you that their network is error free, ask them if they ever sold snake oil! There is no such thing. Error control is pretty simple: if any given layer of the architecture does not like the data it has been given (because of errors in formatting of data, data corruption, old data, etc.), it can send a nasty message back to the previous layer telling it that there is an error. If the previous layer can provide good data, it will. If not, it may need to go back to the previous layer to find good data and, in many cases, it may need to go back to the originator to get a good copy of the data. It is not necessary to traverse all the way up and down every layer of the architecture every time an error is found. Most of the time, errors in corrupted, duplicate, or bad data are cleared up and fixed by the time the data hits the transport layer. After that, it is usually a data formatting problem, which is more serious, as it means that the remote peer protocol (the protocol at the same level as the one that detected the error) is formatting things incorrectly and will most likely require some sort of human intervention to fix the problem, and we all know what that means.

Errors can be caused by interference on the wire (electronic emission interference, magnetic interference, radio frequency interference, bulldozers cutting the wire in two, DC or AC motors next to unshielded wire, etc.), hardware problems in the communications adapters or controllers, or software bugs or other problems that cause corruption of the data between nodes. Some errors are called "intermittent" because they come and go like the wind (and are about as hard to catch). Others are "hard" errors that can easily be tracked down (notice I didn't say easily fixed). Under most conditions with a properly functioning network architecture, errors are usually due to corrupted data packets due to line synchronization failures, packet collisions, and other such items.

Chapter Comments

Network architecture is nothing more than a tiered or layered approach to the implementation of the communications mechanism between nodes. Some architectures follow the seven-layer OSI model, some do not. It does not make one better than another, but it can make each more difficult to understand or to get the dissimilar architectures to work with each other.

Just because a network architecture conforms to the OSI architecture DOES NOT MEAN THAT IT IS COMPATIBLE WITH OTHER OSI IMPLEMENTATIONS BY OTHER VENDORS. That is akin to saying that all implementations of BASIC on different systems are the same. Hogwash! Just as with languages, network architectures can be radically different and must be carefully chosen for your environment.

Your biggest enemy in the communications world is queueing delay. Queueing delay is an elusive thing and difficult to measure (a Ph.D. in Statistics helps, but not much), but it is there and can be estimated. Remember that all network architectures impose queueing delays upon your data while it is in transit and should be monitored closely.

Finally, remember that processors not currently running communications software will be degraded when running communications software. More work is imposed upon the processor and more resources need to be used. In some situations, the communications architecture implemented on the system is more sophisticated than the operating system itself and requires more resources (sad, but very true in a great many instances). Plan for the degradation, choose routing nodes carefully, and always be mindful of queueing delay.

To quote an old Doonesbury saying by Uncle Duke:

"Be firm, fly low, and stay cool."

Chapter Six

Dial-up Networking

INTRODUCTION

Many times, it is more cost efficient to use voice-grade lines and dial-up a remote system for occasional access to remote system resources. In this chapter, we will examine some of the methods by which this can be done.

What Is Dial-up Networking?

Dial-up networking is a term I use to describe the use of dial-up capabilities to set up a network between selected nodes. Traditional networks use, typically, leased phone lines or circuits or, in some cases, public data networks to communicate between nodes. Many times, this is too expensive for the occasional network user and networking to outlying locations can be done much less expensively with dial-up capabilities.

What Does It Take to Do It?

Setting up a dial-up network involves the use of cooperating communications software on the host system and the remote system and compatible MODEMs. For instance, if you are using XYZ software on a remote IBM PC, then the host would have to be running some sort of software that is either XYZ compatible or is a version of XYZ for that type of system. Another method of setting up a dial-up network is the use of terminal emulation software on the remote to make the remote system look like a terminal to the host, or dialed-up, system. In this case, the communication is not as "smart" and error control can be a problem, especially with noisy phone lines. Also, terminal emulation software usually allows simple file transfer capabilities, but may not be set up to check for errors on transmission and other desirable features to insure that the file gets to the host intact. In both situations, MODEMs that are compatible with each other are required on each end of the communications link to allow the remote to access the host.

The Dumb Terminal Situation

To simplify things, let's look at the use of dial-up networking to solve the problem of remote access to mainframe applications by a PC. Let's also suppose that the PC is located in Denver and the host in Dallas.

The first thing to do with any network design is to define what the network is supposed to do. For our example, we will need the following capabilities:

o Terminal emulation of a VT220-type of terminal
o Ability to capture screen data on the PC
o Ability to dial-up the host system automatically
o Ability to use existing IBM PCs in Denver to access the Dallas system

Now that we know what we want the network to do, we need to know what we have to work with:

o **Denver**
    IBM PC/XTs (3) w/keyboard, dual 360Kb floppies, 640Kb mem., etc.
    Serial ports available
    No MODEMs available (yet)
    No communications software
    20Mb hard disk, 10Mb used
    Extended graphics adapter (EGA) card
    Color monitor
    Limited user expertise

o **Dallas**
   1VAX-11/785 w/4Mb of memory
   16 Direct Memory Access (DMA) terminal ports, four available
   456Mb of disk, 300Mb available
   5-7 users on-line at any given time
   10-12 jobs running on the system at any given time
   1 1600/6250 BPI tape drive
   2 Bell 212A MODEMs on two terminal ports for dial-up access
   No communications software
   Applications software uses VT220 graphics sequences
   Applications software can be screen-intensive

It's quite obvious that we have two problems that have surfaced just from the above equipment and software lists: we are missing communications software on both ends and we are missing MODEMs on the PC side of the link.

The initial reaction of most people would be "No sweat! Just add a 212A-compatible MODEM to each PC, put some terminal emulation software on the PC, and let 'er rip." Wrong, buffalo breath. It don't work that way!

Let's consider for a minute some of the unanswered questions that need to be solved before we know what kind of MODEMs, software, and systems requirements we need before we can solve our terminal emulation problem.

1. IBM PC Usage

Even though we have a list of components that are available on the PCs, we still do not know how they are currently being used. Also, we do not know what the purpose is for providing terminal emulation capability as well as the need for screen capture capability on the PC. We do not know if the PCs are all located in the same Denver office or in different locations. We do not know what the current user expectations are from the proposed terminal emulation capability we plan to add (the users may need more than we are providing or may not need it at all). We do not know what kind of return on their investment the users expect from this type of networking arrangement. In short, there are a lot of unanswered questions that are critical to understanding the need, the reasons, and the expectations.

2. Host System Capabilities

It is easy to presume that the host system is capable of providing terminal dial-up facilities from the operating system and that it will not be necessary to purchase separate software for the terminal ports with the MODEMs on them. While on most systems this is true, there are operating systems that require special software for access to terminal ports with MODEMs on them. MODEMs use signals that normal terminal connections do not need and the software that controls the terminal port (call the terminal driver software) may or may not support MODEMs, depending upon operating system support. In the case of the VAX-11/750, using the VMS operating system, the system is capable of supporting MODEMs for dial-up terminals. Always check to insure that the operating system will support dial-up terminals without having to purchase additional software. Also, check to make sure that it does not take an act of Congress to get the system to recognize the MODEM-controlled port. On some systems, a system generation (SYSGEN) is required to allow the MODEM to be used on the terminal port. On some systems, SYSGENs are fairly easy to do. On most, unfortunately, a SYSGEN is a major pain in the foot and can take an incredible amount of time and aggravation before it is capable of supporting the MODEM. So, what seems logical and easy to do can be a major nightmare, depending upon the operating system being used on the host system.

The second problem on the host side is the ability of the system to support additional users on the system. While the VAX-11/750 can handle many users and processes, it is not how many users and processes that is important as it is how much of the system they require to execute. For instance, one person on the host running, say, word processing software is

92

not going to take up near the resources of one person running a simulation program such as NASTRAN or SIMSCRIPT. So, just because there is not a lot of people or processes running on a system does not mean that the system can handle the additional load imposed by new users via dial-up. Examine the typical resource needs that a logged-in user would use and check that against available resources to see if the system can handle the load of the dial-ups.

3. Proper Analysis of the Problem

When we talk about proper analysis, we need to remember chapter 4 and the comments about what makes good network design. Some questions we would want to ask ourselves might include:

o Who is going to be using the PCs to dial up the system?

This has some interesting repercussions. If the users are secretarial personnel, the visibility of the project may not be as great as if the user was the group vice-president in Denver. So, who is using the PCs is important to understanding how politically sensitive the network can be.

Other problems associated with the "who is going to use it" question include the training of the user, how often it will be used, how available the terminal port needs to be to satisfy the user's needs, what kind of problems have been involved in getting the PC operational.

o What kind of loading can be expected from the additional dial-ups?

In this question, we would want to know what to expect on the host in terms of additional loading, additional I/O overhead, system performance degradation, overall usage problems, etc.

o What kind of errors can be expected and how would they be corrected?

Errors and error correction is very important to any network configuration. Errors require that software and/or hardware fix same and retransmit the proper data. In the dial-up arena, error control is usually minimal at best and dial-ups are notoriously susceptible to line noise and other related errors due to the analog nature of voice-grade lines and the general differences in switching systems from the originator to the destination. Typically, any errors that may occur may, very possibly, not be corrected and the user may see garbage on his/her display, lose returned data from the host to the PC, or other problems. If this type of scenario is unacceptable, another method of communication may be necessary to provide error-free communications to the host system and satisfy the user's needs.

o How will updates to the PC software or the host software affect the communications link?

When considering any network, the upgrade of software on any node can affect, positively or negatively, the network. In our situation, we want to make sure that any changes to the software on either end do not adversely affect the communications link. If it should affect it, we would want to know how the link would be affected and plan for such an eventuality. Also, we would also want to allow a backup mechanism where either the host or the remote system may revert to the previous version of software or provide for some other reliable backup method until the problem is resolved.

One of the problems with networking is the dependence upon the network that becomes apparent after use of the resource for a relatively short amount of time. Users usually find the flexibility that a network gives to be very beneficial to their jobs and quickly develop a dependency upon the communications capability. Nothing can be worse than something that "works" and then, through the process to make it "better," breaks.

o Who is going to support the communications link mechanism?

It is very important to understand who is responsible for the support, maintenance, and overall capabilities of the link. It is also important for the users to know who this is as well to preclude any misunderstandings

94

or misconceptions. Support also includes upgrades, question answering, training, applications verification, coordination of upgrades, and many other related tasks.

Mind you, these are but some of the things to be considered in proper network design and implementation of any network. Do not forget that even dial-up communications still make up a network and that no matter the size of the network, proper design should always be done to prevent problems and reduce the risk of implementation.

4. Speed

While the host already has two 212A-compatible MODEMs (300/1200 baud, asynchronous or synchronous), it may be that even the 1200 baud rate is too slow to be useful in a heavy graphics environment. Another modem, the 2400 baud asynchronous Hayes-format MODEM, is becoming quite popular, as are higher speed internal-protocol MODEMs such as 4800 baud async MODEMs and 9600 baud async MODEMs. An internal-protocol MODEM is one that uses its own protocol to provide error-free communications between two similar MODEMs. Internal-protocol MODEMs are different from a situation such as a 212A MODEM in that the internal-protocol MODEMs use a vendor-specified protocol to communicate with each other and the 212A prescribes an industry-standard protocol for the 300/1200 MODEMs that are compatible with the 212A protocol method. As a result, finding 212A MODEMs can be much easier to do than finding MODEMs from multiple vendors that comply with a vendor-specified protocol. The basic danger of using an internal-protocol MODEM is the need to purchase the MODEMs from a single vendor, effectively locking you into a single vendor. While this may not necessarily be bad, it can have repercussions should the protocol MODEM not prove to be popular or the company that supplies the device stops making or supporting it or, worse yet, goes out of business.

Configuring a Terminal Emulation Network Link

Now that we have examined some of the constraints and potential problems, let's look at the practical application.

With the current software and hardware configurations, the following components would be necessary to provide a 1200 baud least-cost to implement capability:

o An EIA-232C or D cable (25-pin connectors) from the MODEM to the PC serial port

o A cable with male RJ11 4-wire jacks to go from the MODEM to the phone plug in the wall to connect the MODEM to the phone system

o The capability to connect the MODEM to the outside phone system in the Denver office. Many offices do not have 4-wire plugs due to the use of PBX systems for phone capabilities. It may be necessary to have the PBX vendor supply a 4-wire jack with access to an outside line or it may even be necessary to have the phone company install a separate outside phone line to allow the MODEM access to the remote system. Check this facet of the problem carefully or you may find that all the hardware is in place, but it is not possible to get out of the office due to a lack of phone line(s).

o Communications software on the PC that will allow emulation of a VT220 terminal. There are quite a few terminal emulation programs on the market that emulate a wide variety of terminals. These can be demonstrated and purchased at practically any store that handles software for the PC being used (in this case, the IBM PC/XT).

o Terminal port configuration on the host system to allow dial-up capabilities. This is a fairly trivial thing to do in the VAX/VMS environment and can be done by the systems manager in minutes.

o Creation of accounts for log-in on the host system. Again, this is a trivial operation by the systems manager. It is not useful to try to access a host system unless it is possible to log in to it.

o Training for Denver users on how to use the MODEM, software, and how to log in and use the remote host system.

In this particular situation, the use of the 212A-format MODEMs is a logical, inexpensive one. 212A MODEM prices are very reasonable and can be found in some places for less than $200.00 (U.S.). Also, there are quite a few communications programs in the $100-200 range that would fit the bill for the communications needs and the chances are fair that there is an available phone line at the Denver facility for at least one system to access the outside world and get to the Dallas facility through dial-up. So, for about $500.00 (not including the phone line), it is possible to provide dial-up capability utilizing existing equipment and resources and presuming a low additional overhead on the host system. If the overhead were high, it might be necessary to add memory, peripherals, or other features to the host to allow for the additional load, which would increase the cost to implement the communications link capability.

With the implementation of the communications link, other costs are going to increase simply to allow for the communications linkage. Costs that will escalate will include:

o Long distance phone. With dial-up networking, costs are associated with long distance communications and they will need to be charged somewhere.

o Software maintenance for PC software. Most vendors will charge a fixed amount per year for maintenance and upgrades of their software (upgrades, enhancements, bug fixes, telephone support, etc.)

o Hardware maintenance for the new MODEM(s)

o Usage of the system. Most systems have to justify their existence; therefore, users are charged "funny money." As a result, the new usage of the system will cause jobs to be delayed (more users, less throughput) and will also use up CPU and I/O time.

o Productivity and support time. Systems management or support personnel will spend, initially, more time answering questions and solving problems for the remote users than before. This can reduce overall productivity and increase the cost to provide overall support to the users of the host and the remote PCs.

In this situation, we see how even a minimal configuration has some not so obvious items to consider. Remember, however, that this configuration has not been properly specified as we have quite a few unknowns that we have not necessarily planned for. The listed configuration has been included to show how the configuration would be installed and the problems associated with the installation that may not be readily obvious.

Setting Up a Dial-up Network for Full Network Functionality

Some vendors have networking software that allows a variety of processors and operating systems to communicate in a true networked method. A true networked environment will typically provide file transfer and conversion, program-to-program access, virtual terminal support, and network management capabilities. You will notice that this is much more complex than the terminal emulation problem, as not only cooperating hardware is necessary, but also compatible, cooperating networking software is required.

Networked PC to Host with Networking Software

In the networked environment, dial-up takes on a whole new meaning in some areas and is the same in others. It is different in that terminal emulation software is fairly unsophisticated compared to the complexity of true networking software. Network software requires that the entire communications session be controlled by a network control program that is accessed by applications and network utilities (programs) to provide the flexibility and power of the network architecture. Another major difference is that terminal emulation, while load-indusive on the host system, does not usually impose the load that network software does. Networking software requires more host computing as it will cause more processing to be done to get the data from the host to the remote and back.

Dial-up is the same in both situations in that many times it uses the same hardware in the asynchronous dial-up situation as the terminal emulation situation. In some networking architectures, the remote system may be much larger than a PC and require a synchronous communications device (which also requires special MODEMs) instead of being able to use asynchronous devices. Also, the method in which networking happens will vary from network architecture to network architecture, but the general idea is still the same.

Chapter Comments

In the dialed-up network environment, there are many things to consider that are the same as in any networked environment. Network design cannot be overlooked, even when considering something as basic as dial-up terminal emulation due to the potential load that can be placed on target systems that was not there before the terminal emulation function was put into place.

Terminal emulation software, by its nature, is not very error-protective. If there is a trashy phone line being used, the terminal session can suffer as a result. If error-free terminal communications is absolutely critical to an application, it is very possible that terminal emulation software and communications hardware is not enough to get the job done.

Networking remote systems to hosts via dial-up is similar to terminal emulation dial-up. The major difference is in the software used. If the dial-up uses asynchronous communications, many times the comm hardware will be the same as the terminal emulation function. The major difference will be much better error control and a much more sophisticated network environment that supports program-to-program file transfer, virtual terminal, and other desirable communications features. With additional features, however, come additional complexity, flexibility, and overhead.

99

Chapter Seven

The Local Area Network Experience

INTRODUCTION

One of the hottest topics in networking is the Local Area Network (LAN). Every major vendor has their own and all will tell you that it is the best that can be bought. All will tell you that their network can be used in any environment, provides practically anything you want, and can be upgraded to any network you like. And, if you can believe that, they also have swampland in Florida for sale.

This chapter will discuss what a LAN is, what kind of components are necessary for one to work properly, functional concerns, installation concerns, and other such useful information.

What Is a LAN?

A LAN, by definition, is a network that is in a small (or local) geographic area. There is a lot of dispute as to what, exactly, defines a small geographic area, but most vendors seem content that the total network length does not exceed five (5) kilometers, end-to-end. This means that the idea of running a LAN architecture from Seattle to New York is not within the definition of a LAN. Not that it can't be done, mind you. At that point, however, is the network still a LAN?

LAN size is measured not only by geographic size, but also by population. Most LANs do not support over 1000 systems per LAN and most are much smaller (30-250 range). This is due to the primary customer of LANs — offices. In the U.S., 90% of all offices have under 30 users (not total personnel, USERS), 98% have under 300, and 100% of all offices have under 3000 users. The average number of users in an office environment is 115, and each office averages a 10'x10' space. Most offices utilize a wide variety of equipment (terminals, printers, file storage, reproduction services (TWX, facsimile), etc.) and most managers want to get maximum productivity out of workers and office equipment as well.

Another facet of LANs is message size. Most offices use short, bursty traffic that varies in size as tasks are done. Most traffic in a LAN environment is 1-100 byte control messages, some moderate messages of 100-500 bytes, and occasional file transfers of 500-100K bytes. Most users are idle much of the time, but when a user wants to use the network, any response time less than two seconds is usually unacceptable.

80/20 Rule

LANs also are the center of a communications premise called the 80/20 Rule. The 80/20 Rule claims that 80% of all communication happens within a given organization and only 20% ever goes outside the organizational walls. In the case of LANs, this can translate, easily, to the fact that of 100% of network resources used by the company, over 80% will be used at the local corporate level and only about 20% of all accountable corporate communications will leave a local level. This is easy to imagine. Take your typical PBX system. In most situations, there may only be 2-5 outside trunk lines but there may be 30-50 extensions internally. Most of the calls that will occur, on a whole, will be internal to other extensions and very few to the outside world. This is how the 80/20 Rule works in networks. Most of the traffic in a network will occur between nodes located in the same local area with only about 20% leaving the local area for other nodes or areas. While it is true that not all LANs will conform, strictly, to the 80/20 Rule, practically all will perform the bulk of networking locally with much less than half of all traffic leaving the local area.

Network Application Dictates Network Type

LANs are also the subject of application vs. type. In all situations, the application that will be services should dictate the type of network. This also helps explain why there are various types of LAN architectures. It's quite obvious that an office-oriented LAN may not have all the functionality that is required for a LAN controlling several blast furnaces in a steel mill or the robotics needs of an assembly line. As such, various LAN vendors offer various LAN architectures to provide for the needs of the various LAN environments. Wide Area Networks (WANs) do not have the variety of offerings that LANs have, but they do not usually have to concern themselves with the data rates, access times, and other needs of the LAN environment.

Speed, Speed, Speed

Another attribute of a LAN is speed. Most LANs run at speeds over 2 million bits per second (Mbits or mega-bits). Some can go as high as 100Mbits, and there are some experimental types (using fiber optics and feptosecond-speed lasers) that can achieve speeds of 10-20 billion bits per second (Gbits or giga-bits). Speed, however, is an elusive thing. Just because a network is capable of sending up to 2Mbits of data does NOT mean that the receiving (or transmitting) stations are utilizing the 2Mbit rate. Each processor on a LAN has speed restrictions on how fast its internal I/O happens and how fast it can send or receive data to its network interface (controller). Even very high speed mainframes may not be able to handle over 1Mbit of data per second, maximum, due to processor architectural restrictions, I/O peripheral speed, processor overhead, operating system overhead, and communications software overhead. Therefore, just because a LAN architecture makes a claim to a certain speed, it is not valid to associate that speed with the actual throughput that will be achieved on any given node or any group of nodes.

So You Think That a LAN Is Cost Effective, Huh?

LANs are also characterized by a fairly reasonable cost to implement. This means that most LANs are architected with cost savings in mind. Most

LAN manufacturers know that they cannot charge as much for LAN interfaces for PCs as they can for LAN interfaces on larger systems. They also are well aware of the market pricing threshholds for any LAN interface and software. Most manufacturers try to relate LAN pricing on a "cost per port" basis, similar to the way that manufacturers try to justify terminal ports. In the networking world, one must be careful with such terminology. A "port" on a network could be a single user PC or it could be a mainframe with 200 users on it. A "port" can also be referenced as an individual program being accessed in a networked manner. If this definition is meant, then does that mean that a system capable of handling 200 simultaneous program-to-program connections will have the same "port" cost of a PC? Some vendors think so. If this were the situation and the cost per port was, say $500.00, then the PC would cost $500.00 to implement and the big system may cost as much as $100,000.00 to implement. If that sounds familiar to you, then you see how many vendors price their "ports" on a network: by how many connections can be handled simultaneously.

The port cost can also be used to the vendor's favor in a different way. By the vendor figuring out, statistically, how many "ports" a large system can handle and dividing the total hardware/software cost of the LAN capability by the number of "ports," the vendor can generate a best-case per-port cost. The vendor could just as easily say that the average number of connections will probably be at least 50% of the total number of simultaneous ports, but that can be bad for marketing, as it does not allow the product to be viewed as cost effective compared to other vendor's products. Let's take the figure we used before of 200 simultaneous connections and see how that can be used to the LAN vendor's advantage. If the total cost for the communications software and network hardware was, say, $15,000.00, then the cost per port would be $75.00. If the PC was able to handle three (3) simultaneous connections and its cost for software and hardware was, say, $750.00, then its cost per port would be $250.00. The vendor could also shift the larger system's per port cost by shifting the number of simultaneous connections from 200 to an average of 60 simultaneous connections and the port cost becomes $250.00 per port on the large system. The vendor then claims that the per-port cost for their LAN technology is $250.00 per port, which is less than their estimated $1,000.00 per port for terminal ports. From the cover of things, that seems like a pretty good deal: about a quarter of the price of a terminal interface, full network capability, and it can solve the file transfer problem that terminals need not worry about. If you can believe that one, they also have an oil well deal in Texas that you won't want to pass up.

In the LAN experience, it is impractical to compare terminal port costs to network port costs. In the terminal situation, it is an all-inclusive cost. In the network situation, it takes two nodes with the appropriate goodies to make the network happen. In our case of the PC to the large system, if our only desire was to connect our PC to the main system, our cost would be $15,750.00 for the network hardware and software. Our per-port charge with three ports on each side connected (six ports or three connections) is $2,625.00. That's an awful expensive terminal port! Even if we had two large systems talking to each other, we still have the problem of communication — it still takes two to tango, as it is said. That means that if we have two large systems, our total cost to implement the LAN is about $30,000.00. Of that $30,000.00, we will probably average about 20 connections simultaneously (unless we have a very active network), which means that OUR per-connection (a connection requires two ports — one on the sender, one on the receiver) cost is about $1,500.00 and our per-port cost is about $750.00, which is a far cry from the vendor's per-port cost of $250.00! Remember that our per-port cost figures do not count software and hardware maintenance, operations support, and myriad other costs that will surface in time.

LANs become cost effective the more they are used. The less usage they receive, the more expensive they are. Unfortunately, the more that LANs are used, the more overhead they generate on the system and end up costing more money in the long run. So, for the flexibility and functionality of LANs, you will pay. A lot.

User Installable?

Many LAN vendors claim that their LAN is user-installable. Some actually are, but most are not. Installing a LAN, under most situations, is not a hard thing to do, but the installation must be methodical and installation instructions must be followed carefully.

A Sample Installation

As an example, let's consider the installation of a small Ethernet LAN. Ethernet is a bus-topology (with branches) LAN that allows a variety of computers and smart peripherals to be connected to a common coaxial spine. Ethernet comes in three basic flavors: baseband (the entire bandwidth of the cable is dedicated to the Ethernet CSMA/CD protocol), broadband (the cable is frequency-multiplexed into many channels and at least two channels (usually) are allocated to Ethernet CSMA/CD protocol), and fiber-optic (which can be baseband, broadband, or, with a high enough fiber bandwidth, can look like both). The most popular flavor of Ethernet is the baseband technique, but broadband versions are gaining speed.

For the purposes of discussion, here are some of Ethernet's specifications for configuration and use:

Speed: 10Mbit/sec
Maximum number of nodes per segment: 100
Maximum length of a single segment: 500 meters
Total number of nodes per Ethernet: 1024
Maximum separation between nodes: 2.8 Kilometers
Protocol used: Carrier Sense Multiple Access with Collision Detect (CSMA/CD)
Distance between node connections: 2.5 meters
Cable type: Shielded coax
Packet size: 64 to 1518 bytes
Connection Mechanism: Nonintrusive cable tap

For the sake of argument, we will presume that the proper network analysis and design has been done and Ethernet was the choice made. We will also presume that the network has two nodes and that the nodes are 10 feet apart, to keep things simple.

In our installation, please keep in mind that the LAN could easily be a token ring, token bus, or any other LAN, for that matter. There are certain nuances particular to Ethernet, but these are few. LAN installation requires certain steps to be taken to insure success and these are common across all LAN architectures. Installation steps for successful installations include:

1. Preparation of the site
2. Cable testing and installation
3. Preparation of the cable for installation of taps and transceivers
4. Installation of taps and transceivers
5. Installation of bulkhead wire assemblies on host processors
6. Host processor preparation for installation of network controller
7. Installation of network controller
8. Diagnostic checkout of installed components
9. Adjustment of system parameters for communications hardware and software
10. Installation of communications hardware and software
11. Configuration of the network database
12. Activation of the network software
13. Testing of network software/hardware
14. Throughput analysis
15. User training
16. Turnover for use

In the following sections, we will examine each of the steps involved in the installation of the Ethernet product on a generic basis. While there are nuances to any product, the important concept to grasp is the steps necessary to install a LAN, not necessarily which one.

1. Preparation of the Site

Site preparation involves the readying of the location where the LAN will be installed. In many places, the biggest problem in the installation is the placement of the cable for the network.

Most office buildings have electrical ducts called wireways or wiretrays. In these ducts all the electrical wiring for the building is placed and it usually runs down the length of most halls or in a gridlike fashion above the main areas of the building. Wireways are also set up to run between floors of a building through the elevator shaft or through strategically-placed holes between floors (usually in closets that contain all the telephone equipment and punch-down blocks). In many sites, the LAN cable will be run down the wireway with the other cables. This is where most troubles begin.

If the computers are located in the same room, the location of the LAN cable is usually not a big deal. If there is raised flooring, the cable can be run under the floor. If there is no raised flooring, the cable can be run above floor as long as it is protected from human interference (such as stepping on it, kicking, running things over it, etc.). In areas where an entire floor may have a LAN, it is necessary to install LAN cable throughout the area of usage. In our example, we will concern ourselves with the installation between systems and not the problems of floorwide LAN cabling. Suffice it to say for now that caution must be exercised when installing cables in wireways due to their inconvenient locations (at times), other cables, and frequent access by electricians and other individuals not associated or knowledgeable about LANs.

In our situation, we will presume the cable to be run under the floor. But, how much cable is necessary?

We know from our specification that the systems are 10 feet apart. We also know that rise distance will most likely be no more than 6 feet above the floor (most computer cabinets are not taller than that) and that we should allow for about 2 foot slack on each end. Add that up and we come to 26 feet of cable. Now, to compound the problem slightly, we know that nodes cannot be closer than 2.5 meters (approximately 8.2 feet). That means that we can tap in three places in the 26-foot segment of Ethernet cable (we only need two places). If we take the measurements from one end, the first tap would be at 8.2 feet, the second at 16.4, and the third at 24.6. While the third tap does not pose much of a problem, the first one might, as it will be 8.2 feet from the end of the cable and that would be under the floor of the computer room. And you thought LAN cabling was simple.

Not to worry. In Ethernet, we have a situation that can help us. Ethernet cabling consists of three cable segments per node that allow a single node to tap in to the Ethernet cable itself. These are:

1. Cable from the controller to the cabinet external cable connector
2. Cable from the external connector to the transceiver unit
3. Ethernet cable itself which the transceiver directly connects to

Most vendors allow the customer to order differing lengths of cable for each segment. Do not get the tapping segmentation confused with Ethernet cable segments. Tapping segmentation is included as part of the method to get on to the Ethernet cable. Ethernet segmentation is taking the Ethernet cable itself and cutting it into separate Ethernet segments.

Therefore, our cabling needs for two nodes are:

o Two (2) controller cables 5 foot long
o Two (2) transceiver cables 10 foot long
o One (1) Ethernet segment 25 feet long

This cabling configuration will provide a minimum cable configuration for our Ethernet network needs.

Following identification of cable lengths, we need to plan for the installation of the cable, the controller, and the software. While all that happens later, part of the site preparation is getting all the parties together and getting decisions made to get the LAN in place correctly the first time.

2. Cable Testing and Installation

Once the cable has arrived, it needs to be tested BEFORE it is installed. In larger LAN installations, it is wise to test the cable while it is still on the reel to insure that the reel of cable is still good. A simple test can be done with a Ohmmeter, but a better method is to use a device called a Time Domain Reflectometer (TDR). The purpose of a TDR is to send electrical pulses down the wire and test for how long it takes the pulses to return. If the pulses take an infinite amount of time, the cable is flawless (electrically) and should work fine. If the TDR says that the cable is 10 meters long, you can bet that there is a break about 10 meters down or there is a short of some kind. In those cases where fiber is used, there is a device called a Fiber Optic TDR (FOTDR or OTDR) that gives the same type of capabilities as a coaxial or other copper cable TDR. Some TDRs allow the user to get a hard copy printout of the cable wave form. This can be very useful in secure environments where it is important to know the number of nodes on the cable, how far apart they are, and if any nodes have been added since the last test. I usually use a TDR to show the cable pullers that the cable is good and that it had best be good when they finish pulling the cable through the wireways. By the way, the common term for this is called "ringing out the wire." After the cable has been pulled, it is a good idea to test the cable again with the TDR to insure that the cable is solid and there are no shorts or breaks.

3. Preparation of the Cable for Installation of Taps and Transceivers

Most LANs connect nodes to the main LAN cable through devices called transceivers (transmitter/receiver). The idea of a transceiver is very simple: it transmits electrical signals to the main LAN wire and receives electrical signals from the main LAN wire and passes them back to the controller. Transceivers are hooked on to the main LAN cable through a connection called a tap. Taps come in two flavors: intrusive and non-intrusive. Intrusive taps are those that cause the cable to be disrupted, totally, while the tap is being installed. A nonintrusive tap does not disrupt any other operations on the cable while the installation is being done. Another benefit of the nonintrusive mechanism is the reduction of active connections on the cable. If the cable is not broken up, there are fewer places for it to fail or to act like an antenna for radio or electrical signals (connectors will do that). In the case of Ethernet, the type of tap used depends entirely upon the vendor. The specification calls for nonintrusive types of taps, but that is not always practical or practiced by vendors. In the case of fiber optics, practically all tapping mechanisms are the intrusive type, but with the use of new selective-light amplification tapping units and transceivers, companies are starting to introduce non-intrusive tap mechanisms for fiber optic cable plants.

Installing a tap on a cable, such as Ethernet, requires a tapping tool of some sort and a flashlight. Tapping tools are usually a manual operation (utilizing a clamp for the cable, an alignment guide, and a screw-in tool that will eat away the shielding and appropriate dielectric at the appropriate depths), but some utilize a drill bit with a battery-powered drill. Many people opt to buy the drill themselves, but, UNDER NO CIRCUM-STANCES, should an AC powered drill be used. If used, the AC powered drill can cause a ground loop throughout the coaxial cable, effectively shorting every transceiver hooked up to the cable. Since some transceivers can cost up to $700.00 each, such a mistake can get very expensive in a big hurry! Use the battery-powered drill and keep the cable happy. Once the hole is made by the drill or the tapping tool, use the flashlight to remove any leftover dielectric, shielding, or braid that may potentially cause static or a short.

Once the tap is ready, it is time to install the transceiver. Transceivers come in various shapes, sizes, and prices, but it is CRITICAL that the appropriate transceiver be used with the correct network controller (on the CPU side) and with the correct cable diameter (on the Ethernet cable side).

Most vendors will only support LAN connections with their own hardware all the way to the Ethernet cable. Mixing or matching to save money will do nothing but cause large support problems in the future, not to mention a lot of finger pointing. The cable diameter is important, as most transceivers for LANs have a cable guide of a predefined size for a predefined cable diameter. If the cable is too large in diameter, the tap for the transceiver (a spinelike protrusion that connects the transceiver to the cable) may not reach the center coaxial conductor. If the cable diameter is too small, the spine may overshoot the center conductor or, worse, cause a cable short by connecting to the shielding or braid on the other side of the center conductor.

Attaching transceivers to the cable is usually pretty simple. Most vendors use an allen-wrench set-up that allows the transceiver to be screwed down into position with few problems. Also, most transceivers have alignment clamps and guides built into the transceiver housing, so it is fairly straightforward to get a transceiver on to a cable.

Once the transceiver is connected to the cable, the transceiver cable is attached. This operation involves the use of the cable that runs from the computer cabinet bulkhead to the transceiver itself. Most transceiver cables use a 9 or 12-pin "D" connector, which is screwed in using a small screwdriver (similar to the way that terminals are attached to EIA-232D cables). When the transceiver cable is installed, use a plastic cable tie (you can get them from any electronic shop or ask your field service engineer — they usually have a ton of them) to connect the hanging transceiver cable to a secure place on the transceiver and another cable tie to secure the bulkhead connection end of the cable to the bulkhead. This will reduce the strain on the connectors and keep an accidental pull of the transceiver cable from ripping apart connectors or causing a fault that is hard to track down (due to the cable being partially connected, etc.).

4. Installation of Bulkhead Wire Assemblies on Host Processor(s)

This step is fairly easy. Most LAN cabling systems use an interconnection point that allows the controller cable to be connected to the transceiver cable. Such interconnects are nothing but a passive (no power) connector block that takes one cable format and converts it to another cable format (such as ribbon cable to 12-wire round cable). Bulkhead wire assemblies are usually attached to the inside open space of a peripheral cabinet, close to the location where the network interface board is located. Installation usually requires a screwdriver and a wrench to tighten any nuts that may be used to secure the adapter to the cabinet.

5. Host Processor Preparation for Installation of Network Controller

On many systems, the installation of new hardware controllers is fairly straightforward. Some network controllers, however, require backplane rewiring or adaptation (such as in the case of direct memory access options on some computer busses) as well as special power supplies due to power loading factors. Your network vendor can give you specifications that are necessary for power, cooling, installation operations, and other requirements that your field service engineer may need to install the device. You will also need to insure that there is sufficient, open backplane space that will allow the installation of the network controller. If there is not, it may be necessary to install additional backplane space, and that can get very expensive. If your system is a small, well- marked machine such as the IBM PC (and compatibles), the IBM System 36, and others, it may be possible to do the hardware installation yourself. In most cases, however, don't get your hopes up too high, as the vendor will most likely need to install the device.

On some systems, devices require a unique system buss address that is usually switch-selectable by the field service engineer during installation. That address is what is used to interrupt the processor during I/O operations and is usually referenced in any driver software that is used to allow the hardware to communicate with the system. As a result, changing the hardware addressing may cause failure of the software. Care must be exercised to make sure that both the hardware and the software addressing is set up for the same address(es). While on the subject of addressing, network components almost always have a network address as well. On some networking architectures, the network address is set in software; on others, it is in hardware. It is very important to find out IN ADVANCE which mechanism your network will use and assign addresses to nodes prior to network hardware installation. Many vendors send their boards preset to a factory address; if all the systems are simply "plugged in" and the addresses are all the same on all nodes, you can imagine the chaotic response that can happen. So, there will usually be a system buss address and a network address, but they are not the same and will usually require some forethought.

In addition to the hardware requirements, there are software goodies to think about as well. Most systems will require the system to be modified to allow the new controller to work properly as well as driver software installed to allow the new controller to work with the operating system. System modifications are usually in the form of a system generation (SYSGEN), which causes the entire system to be rebuilt for the new configuration. On some larger systems, this is a major ordeal and can cause a variety of problems for already functioning components and software. For other systems, a SYSGEN takes, literally, seconds and does not disturb most applications or components. The safest way to prepare for the installation is to presume the worst and hope for the best. That way you are never disappointed. Presume that it will take a while to get the host operating system in shape to talk to the network controller and that the installation will be a major ordeal, as it usually turns out to be anyway.

6. Installation of the Network Controller

If the system has been prepared properly, the installation of the network controller is not that painful. A checklist should have been established for installation and other customers contacted to verify the suppositions that have been made about the installation.

Once the hardware has been installed, it usually will have on-board diagnostics in the hardware that can be invoked through a switch

114

command on the board or through a software utility. Always check out the hardware to make sure that it says that everything is OK. Many LAN controllers have LEDs that allow the user to see if there is a failure or if everything is functioning properly. Check your manuals to see how to make use of the LEDs and what they mean; it can save you a bunch of time later on when the network component fails.

7. Diagnostic Checkout of Installed Components

The golden rule of diagnostics, known as Bill's Law of Diagnostics, is as follows:

"Diagnostics are software and are subject to fail at any time. They also tend to lie. Often."

This means that you, too, can be confused and amazed by what seems like properly functioning hardware ("The diagnostics say everything is fine"), which, in reality, is highly broke. The Corollary to Bill's Law of Diagnostics is:

"Different versions of diagnostics lie differently."

So, diagnostics are only as good as the software engineer who wrote them. Some versions will work better than others, so if you do not like the results from one set of diagnostics, you can most likely try another set and get a different result. And, since most diagnostics are not written by the hardware engineers that built the hardware, you can imagine some of the things that can happen.

For those of you readers who think that I am joking, you obviously have not been around diagnostics very long. Keep laughing — your turn is coming.

Be very wary of new diagnostics. As with any program, diagnostics will have bugs and flaws that will be corrected over a period of time. Like other programs, they are constantly under upgrades or revisions and will have certain versions that will work better than others and some versions without the proper support for the necessary option that you bought for the network.

Diagnostics can be very helpful in tracking down a problem with the network hardware. Some vendors even supply a diagnostic routine that runs on every node and allows the diagnostics on the various nodes to perform a node-to-node checkout of the hardware path (this is one of the best methods of checkout besides the actual communications package being active and working properly). Before you install your hardware, check with other users of the network and ask for their opinion on diagnostics and other troubleshooting tools. Some network technologies are very good; others leave much to be desired. Your risk is reduced when you know the facts up-front.

For the sake of argument, we will presume that the diagnostics work correctly. During the installation, the diagnostics show that there is a fault with the network component and the installation engineer decides that a replacement is necessary. When purchasing the network components, you should have specified a maintenance contract with the vendor. Now is the time to see how well the vendor responds to the problem. Many times, the installer can get another board in 24 hours. In some situations, the vendor will require that the board be returned before another is shipped out. In still other situations, the board will need to be sent out, repaired, and then returned. In all situations, a board will most likely be swapped and will require reconfiguration of the system, temporarily, to overlook the bad board or to configure it out of the system while the replacement is being shipped in.

Board replacement is a funny thing. In most companies, when you buy a component, you are shipped a new board. When the board fails (and it will — it's just a matter of how long), it is usually swapped for a functional board. Did you just put in a new board again? Most likely not. You will probably get a "factory refurbished" board, not a new one. That means that the board was used at some other site, failed, and has been fixed and retested to meet quality assurance standards. Does that mean that the replacement component is subject to failure? You bet. Does it mean that it will fail quicker than the new board? Not necessarily. A lot depends upon the vendor's quality assurance program and the methods used to verify fixed components. Don't panic because you get a used replacement. After all, you are giving the vendor a used board anyway. Do be concerned over the vendor's quality assurance mechanism and check it out before you need it.

8. Adjustment of System Parameters for Communications Hardware and Software

After the hardware is installed and checked out properly, it is usually necessary to modify the system parameters to allow the hardware to be recognized properly and to allow the software drivers to be properly configured into the system. The vendor will usually provide guidelines for this and one of the requirements may involve a SYSGEN (discussed previously). Exercise care with this step and there should be few problems getting the components to be recognized by the system.

9. Installation of the Communications Hardware and Software

While it is true that it looks like we have already taken care of the communications hardware, it is possible that the vendor provides standalone network interfaces that need to be installed after the host controller is installed and functional. Not all LANs are alike and some have some rather bizarre configurations to be implemented.

Communications software comes in a variety of media, depending upon the necessary distribution for the host being tied into the network. For most larger systems, it will be on a magnetic tape in a format suitable to the host operating system or one of its tape manipulation utilities. On smaller systems, the software may come on floppies or small tape cartridges. In any case, you will most likely need to specify the type of

117

distribution that you would like from the vendor when you purchase the network.

Some media is configured on a node-by-node basis. This is done to simplify the installation process and to keep users (and companies) from copying the software on to new nodes that need to access the network. With the installation of a LAN, the network transfer of software is much more simplified than the transfer of software through media distribution such as floppies and tapes. This means that the temptation to "copy it over and install it" is greater in the networked environment and reduces the profitability of the company selling its networking products to customers, not to mention the legal issues involved. Be prepared to specify system configurations to the vendor, as it may require them for creation of distribution kits.

Most communications software is installed either in existing systems directories or in specific directories created by the installation process. Additionally, communications software will usually involve some sort of driver to talk to the hardware, a network kernel that handles all the networking functions, and user interfaces in the form of command parsers, utilities, or program libraries for programming purposes. The software may come prebuilt (in executable form), object form and built on the system, or in source form for customization purposes. In all cases, the network software will require some host installation procedure that will be performed by the software installer (usually the system manager or the user of the network). Such procedures are in the form of installation programs, procedure files, batch files, or written commands that are typed in by the software installer in accordance with directions in an installation guide.

With most software installations comes an installation verification procedure (IVP) or test suite of programs or procedures to check out the software and insure that it has been installed properly and functions as expected. It is very useful to perform all test procedures to insure that the installation was successful and that the components do, in fact, function properly.

10. Configuration of the Network Database

Most communications architectures require that a database be kept on each node for a variety of purposes such as counters, event monitors, error logging, routing, and many other purposes. Some products configure the database themselves upon the initial activation of the network. Others have a program that asks simple questions and generates the database for the user. Still other products require a complete, manual effort on the part of the network administrator. In all cases, a database must be generated so that the network knows who is who, where the various nodes are, what the topology looks like, etc. A database must be configured for every node. This can be an important item to remember as some networks will not allow the nodes to communicate with each other until the network databases have been properly set up and configured.

11. Activation of the Network Software

The last step to activation of the network itself is the activation of the network software. Network software is usually activated as a background process, a batch process, or on-demand (as in the case of PCs). The software is usually activated by batch procedures or by specific network programs that are included in the distribution. Activation of a particular node may cause an "event" to occur on the network and all other nodes may respond. An event is, simply, an action on the network that can change the status or configuration of the network. A new node activating changes the configuration of the network, hence, an event has happened.

12. Testing of Network Hardware/Software

Now that the software and hardware have been installed, all components of the LAN architecture should be tested. Most vendors will include programs for testing the various components and methods of access. Over and above those test procedures, it is necessary for the support group to sit down and get very familiar with the network components prior to

119

allowing users to have access to the LAN. This step is very important to proper support and understanding of the LAN technology. As a rule, the following tests should be done:

o Test all file transfer capabilities with all supported file types. (Most networks support sequential file access, but other support relative files and indexed files as well. Test them all.)

o Test all file types with the various operating systems. Make sure that all possible combinations are tested.

o If the network supports it, try sending multiple files to a single node simultaneously to test network synchronization and access.

o If virtual terminal software is provided, try connecting to the various systems and exercise all aspects of the link software (screen editing, forms, graphics, etc.).

o Write some sample network programs to test the network application libraries as well as verify the programmability of the network for future applications. Many times the library used to generate network utilities is not the same library as distributed to users for programming. Test it out!

o Put any network control utilities through the paces. Use them in a typical environment. Try to break the network. The users will.

o If any applications you are currently using claim to support the LAN you have selected, test them as well. Do it before the users have a chance to do it, to preclude any embarrassing questions or problems.

o Disconnect nodes and verify network stability. Take systems up and down in the middle of network sessions to check error control and recovery. If you can figure out a way to disrupt the network, try it. The vendor may claim that the damage you do is unsupported, but if you know the symptoms in a controlled situation, you can handle the problem when it arises on the live LAN.

Vigorously exercise all components and capabilities of the network BEFORE users get access to it. You will never get the chance to play with the network and test out the various components after that happens due to firefighting, question answering, and support duties.

13. Throughput Analysis

As part of any LAN installation, it is essential to know what the best case throughput will be, the average, and the worst. This is necessary in determining if the LAN is responding properly and data is moving at expected rates. Highly scientific tests are not too useful in throughput testing as when the network degrades, there is no time for a highly scientific analysis procedure. The cry that will be heard is "Fix it!" Users do not care about the hows and whys. All they usually want is to get the functions completed they desire to do and not much else.

Throughput can be measured in a variety of ways. I usually write a small program that sends data across a network as fast as it can to a receiving task and time the results. I then keep the program on all nodes so that I can set up a test at any time I want. Other methods include testing utilizing batch files that show the time and size of a file before transfer and show the time after transfer with a display, if possible, of network counters before and after. So, throughput testing procedures can be complex or simple, but complex is usually not real. Simple is closer to everyday life in the LAN environment.

When testing throughput, take time to set up different test scenarios. Load up some systems and try to access them to see what happens (some networks bomb, some sit and wait, others timeout, etc.). Remember also that topology can be your enemy in a networked environment. If your LAN uses a common routing node for all traffic (like in a central star topology), that single node can degrade the entire network. So, in addition to testing for raw throughput, make sure you know what is affecting the LAN and where throughput bottlenecks may exist.

14. User Training

Users have to be trained. They don't think so, but they really need it.

Users typically fall into two categories: the "I'll figure it out myself" types and the "I'm afraid I'll break it" types. Kind of the yin and yang of users, if you want to look at it that way.

The "I'll figure it out myself" types can be the hardest to deal with, as they feel that they have enough background with the systems that learning the network is not a big deal. They will also be the most difficult to deal with, as they will ask (nay, demand) answers to totally irrelevant questions about what they are trying to accomplish and will raise the roof when the questions are dismissed as trivial or unnecessary. Also, this type of user typically wants a copy of all the documentation, as he/she is somewhat distrustful of the support group and feels better doing it him/herself.

On the other end are those who feel a computer will break when they touch it. They tend to have an inane feel of technology. These are most willing to have you help them along, but they must be weaned from protective support after a while or they will never get over their apprehension of the system or the LAN.

There are those users who fall somewhere in the middle, but, oddly enough, they are fairly rare. These are usually the less panicky, more stable types who take things in stride and provide stability for the environment.

To cover the training needs for most users, the best method is a tutorial approach (with exercises and self-tests) that allows the user to read, try, review, and test him/herself on what was learned. Through this method, support group productivity remains high while the learning curve is being built by the user base. In addition to the tutorial training, periodic classroom training should be done to reinforce the tutorial exercises as well as expand into areas not covered by the tutorial training method. Through a combination of these two methods, users can become proficient in LAN usage in a short amount of time and keep the support staff productive in the process.

15. Turnover for Use

By now, the users have been trained, the support staff trained, applications tested, etc., etc., etc. It would logically follow to declare the LAN usable and available, right? Nope, not yet.

Before the LAN can be turned over, the following need to be in place:

o Problem support mechanism. When it breaks or questions arise, who solves the problems?
o Security administration policies need to be updated for the networked environment. Because LANs, by nature, are somewhat nonsecure, the entire network could potentially be compromised through the actions of a single user on a particular node. If a user with system access privileges were to vigorously attack any network, it would be a matter of time before the entire network and any systems attached to it would be penetrated. A network is only as secure as its least secure node.
o Support and maintenance contracts with the vendor need to be finalized and known to the support group. Finding out where to get help before it is needed is always preferable to getting a runaround when help is critical.
o User guides and manuals need to be produced, copied, and distributed for LAN users. These documents are dissimilar to the tutorials in that they provide ready-reference capabilities to LAN users.
o Management and control procedures need to be established to allow for how the network will be controlled, how upgrades will be done, back-ups and restores, and many other management-related tasks.
o Disaster recovery plans need to be modified to reflect the needs and usage of the network in a recovery operation following a disaster.
o Other related items.

From this list, it is easy to see that LANs involve much more than the technology installation and use. They also involve the management and support of the technology implemented.

Types of LANs

Now that we have seen how LANs are installed and the additional aggravations that accompany them, let's take a brief look at the types of LANs that are available and the basics of their functionality.

When looking at LAN architectures, it is useful to remember the OSI architecture we discussed in Chapter Five. As you will recall, the bottom two layers of the architecture (layers 1 and 2) are used to define the physical link and the data link layers. Most LAN architectures conform to a variety of voluntary network standards that specify methods and protocols for the different layers of the OSI architecture. As we discuss LAN architecture, it will be very obvious very quickly that while the hardware used in the LAN environment usually conforms to standards established for layers 1 and 2, there are very few standard mechanisms for access above layer 2 that are compatible with other network architectures. Therefore, when looking into LANs, you will find a great deal of compatibilities between the hardware components of many LAN vendors. There is little compatibility, however, in any layer above layer 2 in LAN architectures.

In any LAN architecture, it is useful to contact the vendor to find out the intricacies of the LAN itself as well as contacting other customers that are using the LAN and its extensions.

A Sample LAN Architecture — Ethernet

Since we have already spent some time with Ethernet, it is pertinent to understand what Ethernet is and how it works. The reason Ethernet is being discussed is that many of the concepts of how Ethernet works and what is involved with its mechanisms are very similar, if not identical, to structures and mechanisms in other LAN architectures. Also, it is one of the most popular LAN architectures with, quite literally, hundreds of thousands of nodes connected together.

Originally designed by Xerox Corporation in the late 1970s, Ethernet is basically a layer 1 and layer 2 LAN architecture that is used by vendors to implement LAN capability between their own and other vendors systems. "Ether" comes from the old term "luminiferous Ether," which was a "substance" that was originally thought to be the material that composed the heavenly/celestial bodies from the moon to the fixed stars (we all know now that it is not luminiferous Ether — it is green cheese). "Net" is obvious (I hope).

Ethernet comes in various flavors (baseband, broadband — explained earlier) and differing media types (coaxial cable, twisted pair, fiber, infrared, etc.). It allows various types of systems to connect to a common wiring scheme and allow communication between the nodes in a prescribed manner called Carrier Sense Multiple Access with Collision Detect (CSMA/CD). CSMA/CD is usually likened to the old telephone party line concept: various stations are connected to a common cable. A station desiring access to the cable would listen to see if the cable is being used (carrier sense; the multiple access part is multiple stations accessing the cable). If no one was on the cable, the station could dial (address) another station and begin a conversation. After the conversation was established, both sides would continue to listen to the line for information and to detect anyone trying to "cut in" or interrupt (collision detection). If both parties attempted to talk to each other at the same time, both stations usually stopped speaking, waited a random amount of time, and tried again. If a further "collision" occurred, a longer time was waited by one or both stations. CSMA/CD is very similar to this scenario. Computers on Ethernet communicate with each other through a CSMA/CD mechanism.

If a collision happens on an Ethernet network, it is the duty of stations being collided with to back off, wait a random amount of time, and try again. Many times collisions are not detected for a certain amount of time due to propagation delays on longer Ethernets. To avoid this and provide for accurate detection (and correction) of collisions, the Ethernet minimum packet length is 64 bytes (this is long enough to allow detection of collisions on even the longest in-spec Ethernet configuration and also to cover for the propagation turnaround time in longer networks). In the Ethernet mechanism, a node using the network listens to its data going out at the same time that it sends the data and compares the two for accuracy. If the data being heard is different than the data sent, then a collision has occurred and the transmitting node will have to back off, wait, and retransmit the data.

Destination	Source	Type	Data	CRC-32

Ethernet V2.0 Packet Format

Destination	Source	Length	Data	CRC-32

IEEE 802.3 Packet Format

Ethernet and 802.3 Packet Layout

In the Ethernet specification, a packet containing data also contains some other information to get the data to the proper node. If you carefully notice the packet construction, it is very obvious that there are no packet "slots" that allow for other protocol layers to insert their particular information. This is due to the nature of a layer 1 and layer 2 specification: there is no need to define for the upper layers if one is defining only the bottom two. Layer 3 and up (to layer 6 and sometimes 7) are defined by the network architecture that sits on top of the Ethernet and are contained in the data portion of the Ethernet data packet. This concept of the data portion containing all information, including network layer protocols and data, is quite common in LAN architectures and present in almost every one. Therefore, even if there is no data to be sent, the data section of an Ethernet packet is never empty when a packet is sent to another node, as the data section will contain network information pertinent to the destination node or nodes.

126

A valuable capability of the Ethernet LAN architecture is the ability of the LAN to support a variety of upper layer architectures simultaneously. Most vendors implement a generic Ethernet with special purpose software at layer 3 and up. Through this method, multiple network architectures, even on the same machine, can share network controller and datagram services across Ethernet without the penalty of additional hardware purchases and the ensuing aggravation.

The Ethernet specification provides for some interesting capabilities when it comes to multimode network access. Multimode, in this context, means the ability to work in different ways on a network wire. Most networks allow the sending station to directly address a receiving station, send data, and, if the architecture supports it, receive a confirmation of reception. In all cases, to get data from point A to point B, an addressing scheme has to be in place. Ethernet uses 48-bit addresses that are assigned on a vendor-by-vendor basis from Xerox. Through this mechanism, each vendor is responsible for its own range of addresses, which keeps misaddressing problems to a minimum. It also allows vendor software to take advantage of this capability. Most vendors place their addresses for their network interfaces in ROM on the network controller cards that fit in the host processors. Through this mechanism, the user cannot access the network device address that the vendor has inserted in the card. All network addresses, even if there are two controllers on the same node, are unique. This is essential to reduce unnecessary overhead on selected nodes with more than one controller and to preclude "eavesdropping" by other nodes with the same node address setting or to keep two nodes with the same address from responding to requests from other nodes and effectively confusing the entire network. Through the use of fixed network addresses (one unique address for each network controller card), the capability of using singlecast, multicast, and broadcast messages becomes possible.

Singlecast messages are those where a specific node addresses a specific node and no other node listens for the message. A multicast message is a message sent to a address that the network controller cards or software know is an address that really does not exist (physically), but is an address that should be listened to and action taken upon the data that is sent. This is useful in areas where certain types of nodes (such as routing nodes) require specific information that not all nodes may require or want. Finally, broadcast addresses tell all nodes to pay attention to the information being sent and take action upon it when received. In all cases, it is the responsibility of the sender to know the address that is necessary to produce the desired effect and the receiver to know which addresses to listen for. There is usually only one singlecast address per node, there can be many multicast addresses, and usually only one broadcast address for the entire LAN.

Ethernet, for its speed and flexibility, has some drawbacks. First off, error control is limited to a 32-bit Cyclic Redundancy Check (CRC-32). A CRC is, essentially, a checksum character generated at the sending node that is placed in a particular sequence that the receiving node knows about. Upon use of the checksum and reverse computation of the algorithm used to generate the checksum, the checksums should match. If so, then the packet arrived error-free. If not, the packet is bad and is discarded. As Ethernet is a datagram service, it does not provide for requests for retransmission of bad packets — that's the job of the upper layers of the network architecture. The greater number of bits used for the checksum usually implies a finer grain of detection of errors, but this varies with the type of CRC algorithm that is used. While on the subject of error control, another problem with Ethernet is survivability — if a segment is cut, the entire segment stops working (the network is not compartmented). This means that it could take some time to locate the problem (using a TDR) and fix the problem before the network is again functional.

Another drawback of Ethernet is the existence of three "standards" for Ethernet — the IEEE 802.3 standard, the DEC/INTEL/Xerox industry standard, and the ISO IS8802/3 international standard. Originally, the only "standard" was the DEC/INTEL/Xerox standard for Ethernet (also known as the Ethernet V2.0 standard). This standard provides for some vendor-specific items that allow the vendors to provide some additional functionality above the base intention of networking, such as terminal connection systems, shared disk servers, shared printer servers, etc. The IEEE standard emerged as a need to generate a series of standards for LANs that vendors could use to provide medium interconnectivity between dissimilar systems as well as medium independence with future revisions and releases of "sister" specifications. In the case of 802.3, the Ethernet specification was modified for the medium compatibility needs of the IEEE and other vendor organizations. In this modification, the packet organization changed as well as cable diameters and distance capabilities. Also, the IEEE specification allows baseband coax (the Ethernet spec'd cable), broadband coax, and fiber-optic cabling, which are not supported in the DEC/INTEL/Xerox specification. Finally, the ISO IS8802/3 standard is nothing more than the IEEE 802.3 standard that has been blessed by the ISO and granted an international standard number (which makes the IEEE specification an international network standard).

The Importance of the IEEE in LANs

What is important about the IEEE vs. the V2.0 standard is that the Ethernet movement started with the Ethernet specification (then called V1.0) from Xerox, was embraced and enhanced by DEC/INTEL/Xerox, and modified for future functionality and capability by the IEEE and standardized internationally. It is interesting to note that DEC, at least, has announced products that will allow its Ethernet product line to interface to IEEE- compliant networks as well as allow DEC to take advantage of future enhancements to the IEEE series of specifications. The IEEE has announced a series of LAN architectures (discussed below) that allow various types of LANs to be implemented, but all could be connected together, regardless of architecture, through a Medium Access Capability (MAC) called Fiber Distributed Data Interface (FDDI). The IEEE, in conjunction with several major computer vendors, has been working on FDDI MAC for some time now and the final specification should be ready in 1986. Also, several methods to allow nonintrusive taps on fiber have been developed as well as some testing on standards regarding the standard fiber types (graded index is popular) and diameters (100/140 micron seems popular at this time) to be used in LAN architectures. Since the IEEE is tightly hooked into the ANSI infrastructure and, as such, into the ISO infrastructure, acceptance of IEEE standards into the international arena is almost transparent. This means that companies looking into LAN architecture would do well to consider an IEEE-compliant layer 1 and layer 2 network product due to future compatibility needs as well as interconnectivity of media between the different LAN standards that is allowed by standards such as FDDI MAC. Remember that at each layer of the OSI network architecture, more than one protocol is allowed. At layer 1 and layer 2, that translates into more than one type of network medium and access capability available simultaneously on the same node, so keep this in mind when considering a LAN.

Other LAN Architectures

In the area of LANs, there is a great many types of architectures, but two other types, besides the bus architecture, permeate architecture types and deserve some mention: token ring LANs and token bus LANs.

Token ring LANs are nothing more than a ring-topology LAN that allows the various nodes to communicate with each other. The idea is that the source node grabs a free token on the LAN, puts data and a destination address in the token, and sends it on its way. The destination node reads the address, determines if the address is its own, and reads the data if it is. When the token returns to the source, the data is cleared and the token is marked as being free by the source node. There are enhancements to this basic concept, such as the destination node marking a part of the token that the data had been received, multiple tokens on a given LAN, "slots" (groups) of tokens on a LAN, etc., but the basic concept of passing the token node to node is the same. The benefits of the token ring method are an efficient usage of bandwidth, stable behavior during high-load times (this is predictable as the stations are all certain distances away, the queueing delay is constant, and the access times are usually constant), and priority scheduling can be implemented on LANs requiring priority message service, something fairly difficult to implement in the LAN bus

130

architecture scheme. Token rings have problems in that it may take an inordinate amount of time to get a token. They usually require special recovery procedures when a net fails or when the network becomes "confused," it can be difficult to add new stations, and the basic topology of a ring is somewhat unreliable due to a variety of factors. Token ring networks that are popular, however, have managed to overcome many of their drawbacks and allow a great deal of bandwidth over short distances as well as allowing a variety of nodes and applications to work well in the given environment. Token rings are very popular in the IBM environment, especially in the areas of office automation (IEEE 802.5) and personal computer networking.

Token bus networks are similar to token ring networks. From a physical point of view, however, they resemble bus topology networks such as Ethernet. Token bus networks are useful in that they provide a predictable access time, ease of station addition, priority scheduling of messages, and become more efficient as more stations have traffic to send. They have problems with inefficiency when there is low traffic usage, are complex to initialize, and experience unusually long delays in obtaining token(s) when transferring data to the load of virtual access. If you have been following the industrial automation folks for the last year or two, you are probably already aware that the token bus architecture (IEEE 802.4) is used by the Manufacturing Automation Protocol (MAP) for control of industrial and factory automation processes.

Chapter Comments

In the LAN experience, it is important to not only choose the right LAN architecture for your corporate needs, but also the right upwardly-mobile technology. In the future, LANs will be based on a variety of media, but the most popular will be broadband coax, broadband fiber, and twisted pair copper media. These predictions are not made lightly, but are done based upon known technology vendors, the IEEE, ANSI, ISO, and other organizations are working on. In some situations, a variety of different types of LAN architectures can be run on the same wiring scheme (one architecture type at a time) with a variety of network architectures perched on top of the LAN layer 1 and layer 2 architecture. Therefore, in companies looking into new building cabling, consider the usage of the more popular LAN media, but always consider the up-and-coming media for future compatibility.

LANs will continue to expand and increase the functionality in the office, manufacturing, industrial, and many other environments, including the home. The International Electrotechnical Commission (IEC) is currently working on a specification (which will most likely be adopted by ISO as an international standard) that will allow a twisted-pair LAN in a home. In the IEC scenario, many appliances and other services (such as voice, medial alert, fire alert, security, Videotex, and others) could be provided on a small, high-speed computer network to control an entire domicile. This can have other implications when considering the Integrated Services Digital Network (ISDN) can be used to connect the various home LANs into various sites. In the future, it may be probable that you can send electronic mail to your home from your office LAN or any hotel in the world. You could potentially control appliances remotely (turn on the lights and stereo from Bermuda while on vacation), have a security service monitor your home, have the LAN dial the fire department in case of a fire, and many other services. LANs, while becoming popular, will be the rage in the 80s, 90s and beyond as the price drops and the need for distribution of information becomes more apparent and necessary.

Chapter Eight

Digital Network Architecture

INTRODUCTION

There are a lot of network architectures in the networking world, but few have the features and capabilities of the Digital Network Architecture (DNA) from Digital Equipment Corporation (DEC). In this chapter, we will discover some of the basic features of the architecture and of the most popular implementation of the architecture, the DECnet network product.

Some History

In 1974, Digital Equipment Corporation decided to develop a communications and network architecture that could provide communications facilities between DEC systems to help leverage machine sales to current and potential customers. The product, later called DECnet, was based upon an architectural model called the Digital Network Architecture (DNA). Through the use of a common architecture, Digital hoped to offer communications capabilities and facilities between dissimilar processor architectures and dissimilar operating systems in a cohesive way.

A further decision was to release the DECnet implementation in phases. It was recognized early on that keeping track of software version numbers on different systems was already a problem. Adding the complexity of making sure that the right versions of network software were on the right versions of the various operating systems would horribly compound the configuration problem. To solve some of the issues involved, Digital began the usage of "phases" of network software release with a certain level of functionality being imposed on each phase. Nodes (systems) on the network that contained the proper level of functionality described in the

133

phase specification could easily converse with other nodes in the same phase of product release, regardless of operating system or hardware involved. Through this mechanism, the confusion as to what version of what needed to be configured was radically reduced.

Each phase of DECnet prescribes three distinct types of issues:

1. The operating systems supported by the phase
2. The communications hardware supported by the phase
3. New features introduced in each phase

Through this mechanism, dissimilar operating systems and computing hardware could be properly configured and activated once the proper DECnet product for that phase was available. Also, as products became obsolete, they could easily be identified for nonsupport and deleted from future phases.

Another benefit of the phase mechanism is the Digital decision to have a newer phase of the DECnet product support the immediately previous phase. This allows a period of time in which two different phases of the software would be totally compatible with each other and allow a migration period to the new phase.

DECnet is what is known as a peer-to-peer network product. This means that no one node is the "master" node. No one node controls or owns the network. All nodes may converse with all other DECnet nodes if they provide the proper access control information and other types of information necessary to support the communications link between the nodes. This type of architecture makes networking very flexible and easy to configure as major software and hardware changes and updates are not usually necessary to add nodes to the network or reconfigure the network topology. The down side is that it is difficult to manage a peer-to-peer network due to the lack of centralized authorization facilities and the need to poll nodes on the network for link, performance, and other pertinent pieces of information. This can cause not only a heavy burden for the system manager but, if network tools are introduced that issue the polls to other nodes, the overhead may increase markedly on the network.

To understand properly why DECnet and the Digital Network Architecture have evolved to where they are today, it is useful to understand the evolution to date.

Phase I

Originally offered in 1976, DECnet Phase I was intended to supply basic file transfer needs and, hopefully, task-to-task communications. For those of you who were around during those early, trying days of DECnet Phase I, you deserve undying admiration and sympathy. Phase I left much to be desired and did not conform to the standards that it does today for the simple fact that the standards did not exist. Most of the standards that DECnet conforms to today were started around 1978, and those standards were incorporated in the Phase II DECnet product and subsequent releases. But, just like most "new" ideas, DECnet was growing in a positive direction and has achieved stature because of it.

In addition to not conforming to network standards, Phase I of DECnet only supported the simplest of asynchronous communication hardware and only allowed few nodes on a Phase I network. Routing was not available, so all nodes wishing to converse had to be directly connected to each other, seriously stifling the network configuration possibilities. Few operating systems were supported (such as RSX-11D and IAS on the PDP-11 line of processors and the short-lived implementation of DECnet/8 on the PDP-8E) and little expertise at Digital and at customer sites compounded problems for all.

My experience with Phase I was an unhappy one. Many a time my systems suffered bizarre system crashes and extreme degradation of the processor due to DECnet problems. Most of these problems were fixed in Phase II, but to say that Phase I had problems would be a large understatement.

Phase II

Phase II introduced closer conformance to the International Standards Organization (ISO) Open Systems Interconnection (OSI) Architecture standard. It also introduced numerous bug fixes and a bit more documentation to reduce the "magical" quality of DECnet. It was also the first release where all PDP-11 and DEC-20 operating systems actually communicated in a reasonable fashion. File transfers actually transferred, task-to-task communication was possible, and the concept of manual routing was introduced. Basically, to get from node (system) A to node C through node B, one had to enter explicitly the nodes through which the message was to travel. Considered a "poor-man's router," it did work, and thus basic routing capability was formed.

In addition to fixing most of the problems with Phase I, many more operating systems were added to the supported list. TOPS-10, TOPS-20, RSX-11M, RSTS/E, RT-11, and others could become members of a DECnet network. Towards the end of the Phase II product life, the VAX was introduced and support for Phase II was introduced as an add-on product for the VMS operating system.

Phase III

Phase III DECnet provided full routing functionality, expanded task-to-task capability, expanded file support capabilities, closer adherence to standards, and, on RSX-11M (initially), a new feature — alternate link mapping. Alternate link mapping is a technique used that allows DEC nodes on dissimilar types of networks (one, say, on an X.25 network and another at the end of a DMR-11) to communicate by letting the lower protocol layers figure out where the remote node was and change the message to the proper protocol or device to allow transparent communications. This began the era of usage of DECnet on "foreign" networking technology instead of the traditional DDCMP (Digital Data Communications Message Protocol) protocol-oriented nets. Now, customers could have

136

nodes connected to public packet switched networks (PPSNs — e.g., X.25) and to traditional DDCMP-oriented networks and communicate between each other using the same user interface.

Phase III also gave customers the concept of remote (virtual) terminals. A remote terminal is one where a user "sets" him/herself to a remote node and logs in as if the remote node were the host. A communications package on a PC is very similar to a remote terminal. Basically, the user starts up a program on the host system and it initializes network communications with a remote program on the remote node. This program creates an "environment" that looks to the remote system as if the incoming network connection is just another terminal. This allows the user at the host to do anything at the remote he or she could if he or she was directly connected to the host via MODEMS or cables. While some of the capabilities existed in previous phases of DECnet, this was the first phase where such work was accomplished in earnest.

Another important feature of Phase III DECnet was the introduction of transparent programming capabilities on VAX systems. Previously, to communicate across the network under program control, one had to use a special library of calls to DECnet to transfer data. A typical exchange would be to "open" the network, "connect" to the remote node, send and receive data, "disconnect" from the remote node, and "close" the network. This type of programming, while not overly hard, could get somewhat confusing and usually required a fairly detailed knowledge of network operations and architecture on the part of the programmer. With the advent of transparent programming capabilities (on VAX systems ONLY), DECnet is a breeze to use when communicating task-to-task. The programmer simply "opens" a remote node's communicating program just as one would open a file. The remote program is then treated as a sequential file and simple read and write operations are used in the language preferred, thus precluding the need to have a detailed understanding of networks and their many idiosyncrasies. For instance, a FORTRAN program would open the program at the remote node with an OPEN statement, write to the program with a WRITE statement, and read data from the remote node with a READ statement. Another important feature of DEC-net Phase III was the inclusion of DECnet in the VMS V3.0 executive. Now, instead of a layered product that "sat" on top of the executive, the DECnet "executive" was made integral with the VMS executive, thus improving throughput and increasing ease of use and functionality.

Probably the most important feature of the Phase III release was the implementation of full routing. Instead of having to figure out which node to go through to get to a remote node, the network routing database takes care of all routing duties. With the support of 255 nodes in the routing algorithms, flexible networks could now be configured and used.

DECnet Phase IV

DECnet Phase IV appeared on doorsteps in the fall of 1984 and has some enhancements that make the DECnet architecture closer to the ISO OSI standard and more compatible than ever. Inclusion of Ethernet support and, for VAX customers, the computer interconnect (CI) in the lower layers of the architecture, Phase IV, like its predecessors, retained "backward" compatibility with previous Phase releases, insuring that functioning networks will continue to do so.

Of significance, over and above the support for the Ethernet LAN, was the support for Phase IV DECnet on the Microsoft MS-DOS operating system for the PC as well as the DEC version of UNIX, Ultrix. While the support for the PC was expected, it is interesting that it was supported due to the fact that the operating system is not a DEC-provided and supported operating system. This marked a change for Digital, providing a DEC product on a non-DEC computer and non-DEC operating system.

Third-party vendors began to offer DECnet Phase IV compatible systems for non-DEC supported systems and operating systems. TCI introduced DECnet for MS-DOS and various versions of UNIX (through their CommUnity product series); Thursby Software Systems (TSS) introduced TSSNet, a DECnet implementation for the Apple Macintosh; and other companies began to offer products for other non-DEC environments. At the end of March 1988, there were an estimated 16 different operating systems supported through a DEC-provided DECnet product or a compatible third-party product.

Phase V

In December of 1987, Digital announced support for DECnet Phase V. Phase V is a new evolution in the DNA realm, as it fully supports the OSI model, including usage of OSI protocols at all layers, where reasonable and supportable. The intent of Phase V is simple: provide the look and feel of DECnet, but do so using all OSI protocols and capabilities, thereby making DECnet a true OSI implementation and able to converse with other OSI-based systems. An ambitious goal, Phase V is being implemented in stages over the next three to five years and will eventually be entirely OSI compliant.

While it seems that Phase V is just another phase of network architecture for DNA, it is much more. To implement Phase V and retain compatibility of user interface and "feel" is very difficult. Further, the need to support completely dissimilar communications protocols and routing algorithms from any previous implementation requires a massive recode of the architecture on selected operating systems. Another issue is which operating systems to support with Phase V capability and which will be summarily "dropped."

Phase V DECnet provides additional functions besides OSI capabilities. It supports a distributed naming service, distributed file service, distributed queueing service, File Transfer Access & Management (FTAM), Virtual Terminal Protocol (VTP), domain networks (with subareas), generic management protocols, and other capabilities. Support for domains also requires a recode of the addressing scheme to support the expanded addressing need. In DECnet Phase IV, node addresses consisted of a 16-bit address that contained the network node address and node area. In the OSI addressing scheme, a 20-octet address is used with six of the octets being used for a specific node (48-bits). Through this method, extremely large networks can be supported.

Now that we have seen a little of DECnet's growth and functionality, let's look at what makes DECnet tick.

How Does DECnet Work?

DECnet is implemented on DEC machines as a Layered Product (with the exception of VAX/VMS). This means that to get DECnet on your processor, you have to contact your smiling DEC salesperson and he or she will sell you a license to operate DECnet on your system and a distribution (media) kit if you so desire. Frequently, in a multinode site of similar machines, only selected machines will get a fully-supported license and all remaining networked machines will get a license to operate. This reduces the implementation cost of networks substantially and also the number of distribution kits floating around the shop. It is not usually a good idea to get one distribution kit for a large, multinode network that is located in different locations. This leads to network update delays, support problems, and other intangibles that have to be seen to be believed. Remember also that a RSX-11M DECnet distribution kit will NOT work on a RSTS/E system. Get the right kit for the right operating system. If you are a VAX user, you will get a DECnet "key" from Digital to unlock the transport layer (described below) and allow node-to-node communications. DEC frowns greatly upon "purloined" copies of DECnet, so get a license and keep it legal.

DECnet consists of a set of layers that communicate with each other (hence the term "layered architecture") to provide communications functionality. Each of the different layers uses a different type of protocol and has a different type of functionality. As user and program requests travel down the layers of DECnet, the proper information is placed in a packet that will exit the node and travel to its final destination. Additionally, incoming packets travel up the protocol layers until they reach their target program or user interface. The exception to this rule is the packet that is being routed to another node. It travels up the architecture to the session control layer. In the session control layer and the transport layer the routing databases are kept and in turn determine where the packet is to go. The determination is made and the packet is sent on its way to the next node whether it is the final destination or another routing node that will help the packet reach the final destination.

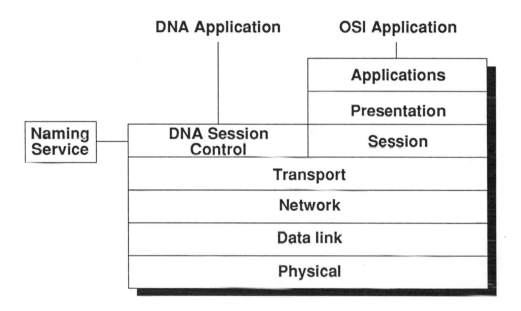

DECnet Phase V Architecture

The bottom three layers of the Digital Network Architecture (or DNA, as DEC likes to call it) are the ones that get the real workout. At the lowest level are the DECnet hardware interfaces. These interfaces hook up to local area network cables (Ethernet and CI), modems (DDCMP devices such as DMR-11s and X.25 devices such as the KMS-11/BD), or local wire/coax connections (DZ11s, DL11s, DMR-11s, etc.). On some hardware, such as the DEUNA/DEQNA interfaces for Ethernet, the actual network protocol is built and stripped at the hardware level. Therefore, little information about the actual communications protocol is necessary in the

141

layers of the DECnet product. In some situations, however, this is not entirely true. In the usage of serial, asynchronous communications (such as DZ11 to DZ11 on PDP-11 systems), the protocol may be implemented in software to ensure error-free delivery of communications packets. The transport layer works to get the data out of the correct interface and the session control layer gets the data to the correct node. Even if users on a given node are not sending or receiving anything, if the node is a routing node (not all nodes are; this is dependent upon the network configuration), it may very well be doing a great deal of work that is unseen by the user community. It is felt, however. To do processing, a program requires access to the CPU; this means that a very active routing node can degrade overall processing capabilities at the node to a great degree, depending on the volume of routing traffic, processor power and capability, and tuning of the system.

DECnet has two databases that are critical to its functionality: the permanent database and the volatile database. The permanent database is used to store static information concerning the node and its interfaces as well as network program states when the node is "turned on." This can be interpreted as "this is who I am and what I can do and access" type of information. The permanent database is read by the network loader upon initialization of DECnet at the node and loaded into memory tables. The volatile database is the memory-resident table(s) that is created after DECnet is initialized and is used for all information until the system shuts down or until the network is stopped at the node. The volatile database keeps track of interface status, the routing matrix, adjacent node status, and counters. Both databases are easily modified by the system manager of the node in question through network utilities.

When DECnet is "turned on," this starts an endless chain of HELLO and TEST messages that are passed around the network when things are idle to ensure network integrity. If an adjacent node doesn't answer the messages within a predetermined time frame, it is considered unreachable and the database is updated to reflect same. When the node is activated again, it will answer the messages and the status will change to reachable. This continually happens throughout the life of DECnet on the node.

Just like anything else that is built by humans, DECnet and its components (hardware and software) occasionally break. When this happens, the system manager/user has a few tools at his disposal to help resolve the problem. Loopback testing is the technique that is used to test faulty components. A program is initiated on the node that tries to talk to a receiver task either on the same node or on other nodes. Think of it as a flashlight trying to find a mirror to reflect in. At each level, there is a mirror that can be activated to reflect the "light" until the reflection does not happen. When this occurs, the faulty component has been isolated and repairs can take place.

Installation of the DECnet product is not terribly difficult, but care must be taken to ensure that all nodes on the network are configured properly to get the best possible performance. On PDP-11 and DEC-20 systems, DECnet can be installed in about an hour by a person experienced with layered product installations and some communications background. On VAX, it takes about 30 minutes to get everything configured correctly. It is important to note that things like network data packet sizes should be the same on all nodes to prevent needless processing and potential problems. Little things such as this can cause performance problems, but to bring up DECnet, provided the hardware is installed correctly, not much has to be done.

At the user level, DECnet communicates with remote nodes through DEC-supplied utilities. VAX people have it pretty easy — most of the DCL commands have DECnet functionality imbedded in them. PDP-11 people are not so lucky. Utilities such as NFT, the Network File Transfer utility, are supplied to allow DECnet user functions. Don't let things like NFT frighten you. The utilities have the same functionality and syntax as already established utilities such as PIP. They require little training and are fairly straightforward in their use.

As can be seen, DECnet can help expedite information transfer and increase system flexibility. But, it does have its problems.

With any processing environment, security is an issue that most system users and managers are plagued with and assaulted with from all sides. Implementation of a network, ANY network, will not help solve these problems. If anything, it will compound them. DECnet assumes that it is operating in a nonhostile environment; hence, it has little in the way of security features. Granted, not many folks would be so industrious as to place a protocol analyzer on a phone line to get information as it passes from site to site, but this can happen. Additionally, the network is only as secure as the least secure system. If a single system has poor security and audit control, that system is a potential target for network exploitation. Users of DECnet are cautioned to tighten up system security on network nodes as exploitation over the network is difficult to trace and is possible.

Probably the most aggravating problem with networks is that they break. As discussed before, it is possible to repair a network, but it is also necessary to know how it works. This means that trained network specialists are frequently needed to fix broken networks and, needless to say, they can be difficult to find. Expertise in system and network architecture, communications theory, protocol design and implementation, use of analyzers and other debugging tools, communications component design (MODEMs, switching centers, etc.), programming, etc., are necessary qualities for the trained network analyst. Frequently, the network analyst will use most of these tools to fix the broken network and get it back up and running in a minimal amount of time. There are the times, however, that all the expertise in the world will not help and that is usually when one is dealing with the phone company. Those who have not experienced dealings with the phone company have not know true, unadulterated anguish. And now, with the divestiture of the "only" phone company in town, such headaches are compounded. For example, moving a data channel from one location to the other is the responsibility of AT&T. Moving the MODEM is the responsibility of American Bell. AT&T doesn't always tell you such neat things, so you wait for the MODEM to be moved, but it is not. After frustration sets in, calls to AT&T reveal (weeks later, of course) that American Bell is supposed to move the

MODEM. Why were you not told? "You never asked, buddy." Therefore, a network analyst understands the most brutal entity in the communications chain — how to deal with the phone companies.

DECnet is not for everybody, but neither is jogging or karate. Selection of the DECnet product for your environment needs to be from the result of many hours of traffic analysis, cost analysis, support staff identification, and needs analysis. But, for the flexibility, timeliness, and functionality, DECnet is tough to beat.

Chapter 9

Systems Network Architecture

INTRODUCTION

IBM has a networking product that they have invested a great deal of time
and money into. It is somewhat expensive, difficult to configure, difficult
to change, but it DOES work and has some interesting features that are
useful to understand.

Called Systems Network Architecture (SNA), it is a networking product
and a philosophy of networking at the same time. In this chapter, we shall
discover a bit more about it and what it means to networking.

Some Background

SNA started off in 1974 as a means of extending the host architecture of
IBM mainframe systems. In 1978, it underwent a fairly drastic revamp to
allow true networking capabilities and was again overhauled in 1984 to allow what IBM calls "a system of networks." A "system of networks" is
basically the allowance of smaller, private networks (such as token ring
LANs, terminal networks, etc.) based upon differing technologies, to be
interconnected into a larger, more distributed network. IBM tends to view
the overall network topology as a large distributed system, hence, the term
a "system of networks."

A Comparison

As you are probably already aware, DEC likes to compare the DNA to the
Open Systems Interconnect (OSI) Reference Model on a regular basis. As
you are also aware, Digital supports multiple technologies at layers 1 and

2 of the model (such as Computer Interconnect (CI), Ethernet (NI), DDCMP (async and sync), X.25, and others), which utilize multiple base protocols. For instance, CI uses SCS protocol to communicate; Ethernet utilizes various protocols such as MOP, LAT, CTERM, and others. The issue at hand is that there is no one singular protocol at layer 2, specifically, that DEC claims to be "the" protocol for use on all processors. This is because DEC wants to support multiple protocols at all networking levels and wants to encourage networking of dissimilar machines and use the latest network technology, where reasonable.

Well, IBM has a somewhat different view of the computing and network world. While SNA is implemented in layers, such as OSI, the layers do not represent the same meanings as the OSI labels except for layers 1 and 2. Regardless of the layer 1 hardware, at layer 2 the preferred protocol that is "the" protocol in the IBM world is SDLC, or Synchronous Data Link Control protocol. This means that if you want to talk to most SNA supported devices, you had better be able to speak SDLC. IBM views this as a feature as it provides a single, uniform line discipline that is predictable, stable, and implemented on a wide variety of processors. IBM can get away with it as well. When you own 70% of the computing marketplace, it is fairly straightforward to dictate how conformance will be handled. So, DNA looks at being able to support multiple lower-level technologies and protocols. SNA supports SDLC as the primary protocol and is starting to allow connection of other network technologies, such as the token ring, but still supporting SDLC as the main access protocol at layer 2.

At the host level, the DNA architecture differs from the SNA world in a radical way. In DNA, there is no "master" node — all nodes are equals in the eyes of the network. If a node goes down, for whatever reason, it does not necessarily "kill" the network or cause a catastrophic condition on the network. Even in the Ethernet environment, if the only router on the segment (which would also happen to be the Designated Router) were to die a miserable death, the end-nodes would still continue to communicate without the use of the router. SNA is philosophically different. A central point of control (called a Systems Service Control Point — SSCP) in a group of nodes (called a DOMAIN) controls all connection requests and network flow. SSCP services are typically provided by mainframe-resident access services. Upon establishing the SSCP in a domain, all control to nodes in the domain is then hierarchical — every critical transaction to the communications process must be controlled by the SSCP. The most common mainframe-resident SNA access method is called VTAM or Virtual Telecommunications Access Method. An older access method called TCAM (Telecommunications Access Method) is still around on some nodes, but IBM does not push its sale and it requires an extremely technical and competent staff to manage it, as it is difficult to configure, maintain, and use. VTAM provides a means for host-resident programs, queues, etc., to gain access to remote facilities on an SNA network in a manner similar to the way that DECnet allows user programs and utilities to access other nodes and resources. The similarities stop there, however. VTAM controls the access from unit-to-unit in a domain. It has to know who is where, what services they provide, etc., through system generation and parameter tables that are located in various parts of VTAM and in 370x network controllers. The end result is that if the mainframe that has VTAM running on it dies, for any reason, new connections may not be able to be done and other networking functions will suffer. In the DECnet environment, connections to other nodes continue unabated (unless the node that dies is a routing node, but that will cause problems in both networking technologies). IBM, realizing the weakness of host-resident network control, is coming out with a new version of Network Control Program (NCP) software for the 370x-series of network controllers called NCP/VS. NCP/VS's main purpose in life will be to provide mini-SSCP services for some connection requests and to offload some of the SSCP functions that a host typically has to make down to the network controller level. This will have the effect of reducing connection dependency on the host and also speeding up some of the connection access time between entities on the network that wish to connect with each other.

Network Space

SNA views entities in the network space as being Network Addressable Units or NAUs. A NAU is nothing more than an IBM term that means that all items capable of working together in a networking environment, both at the physical and virtual levels, have a method of being selected for access. To do this, SNA assigns designators to functions that physical devices or programs provide. A Physical Unit, or PU, provides physical connectivity between devices. Every node on an SNA network contains a PU and can be accessed by the SSCP for the domain in which the PU lives. Programs, as a rule, do not establish connections to PUs, as they provide level 1 and level 2 network capabilities that are of interest only to the networking system (i.e., SSCP or another PU wishing to downline-load a PU). PUs (and all other NAUs) are characterized by "what" they are capable of doing through the use of PU TYPE designators, as follows:

PU Type 5   -   Physical unit in a subarea node with SSCP (VTAM or TCAM node)

PU Type 4   -   Contained in a subarea node without SSCP (37x5 controller)

PU Type 3   -   Not defined

PU Type 2   -   Peripheral node PU, such as a remote system, terminal, etc.

PU Type 2.1   -   Enhanced PU Type 2, which will supersede PU T1 and PU T2

PU Type 1   -   Support in a 37x% to support single terminals such as 3767

Through the use of PU TYPEs, a network management service can quickly determine if the connection being requested to the PU is legal, capable of doing the job desired, and who has control over the PU, all critical items in a hierarchical network. This also allows for quite a bit of flexibility — it does not matter what the physical hardware looks like or how old or how modern it is, only that it conform to the rules of being a certain PU TYPE and connect into the SNA network.

At the virtual level, SESSIONS (connections) are established to NAUs called Logical Units (LU). A Logical Unit is used to connect end-users (such as program to program or program to network service, etc.); an end-user, in IBM terms, could be a program, terminal, terminal controller, or other "smart" entity. How a session will be run is established at the time the session is created and a BIND command is sent to the SSCP. The BIND command is very important in the SNA environment as it defines how the session will be handled, what services will be used, security issues (such as cryptographic services), etc. A BIND command, in its fullest form, can contain over 30 parameters that must be provided for the session to be properly set up. LUs issue connection requests and, upon approval by the SSCP, a BIND command is issued and the session is underway. Just as with PUs, however, LUs are subject to TYPE restrictions and have their own TYPEs:

LU Type 0   -   Defined by the implementation (can be creatively used)

LU Type 1   -   Application programs-to-device communications to access nondisplay types of devices such as printers, hardcopy terminals, SNA character streams, etc.

LU Type 2   -   Application program communications to 3270 display terminals

LU Type 3   -   Application program communications to printers utilizing a subset of the 3270 data stream

LU Type 4   - Application program communications similar to the services provided by LU T1

LU Type 6   - Interprogram (program to program) communication that
   & 6.1   is SNA defined and part of the new distributed operating system function

LU Type 6.2 - Usually called "Advanced Program-to-Program Communication" (APPC). This is basically a generalized task-to-task interface for general purpose data transfer and communication

LU Type 7   - Application program communications to 5250 display terminals

In the areas of LUs, there are three types of LUs: non-SNA specified (LU0), terminal access LUs (LU types 1, 2, 3, 4 and 7), and program-to-program LUs (types 6, 6.1, and 6.2). To complicate things even more, LUs have "qualifiers" that are imposed at the BIND command that determine how data is represented to the destination LU, what kind of presentation services will be provided, and what kind of transmission subsystem profile may be used. When programming in the SNA environment, these features can be very useful when moving applications from one display class to another as it will allow porting of applications from one LU type to another with minimal modifications if the application is coded carefully to start with. As a result, the use of the data stream "qualifiers" to LU connectivity can be a real help in the high-transaction, large-terminal environments that mainframe systems are usually involved with (2000+ terminals on-line simultaneously).

Network Topologies

Topologically, an SNA network does not look much different than a DNA network, but traffic-wise there are substantial differences. IBM is a company that utilizes the "divide and conquer" mentality quite well and provides "smart" clusters of terminals or network concentrators as cooperating entities in the SNA environment. This means that terminals that are smart can be directly connected to; terminals that are dumb can have a terminal concentrator hooked up to them and the concentrator can be connected to SNA. For optimization of line usage and traffic flow, network controllers can be used to connect multiple terminal clusters or other network controllers together, providing flexible networking configurations that can be changed as growth requires without necessarily replacing existing hardware. Also, since all nodes on the network can be addressed by "names," the reconfiguration of a network, properly done, does not affect application programs that have been written for the SNA environment. Application programs still call the service by "name" and it magically happens as long as the proper VTAM tables and NCP tables have been updated to reflect whatever network changes have taken place.

SNA networks are not limited to a single domain, either. SSCPs can provide session connections across domain boundaries ("cross-domain" session) to requesting LUs, effectively providing large network connectivity with segmented network management facilities. To do this requires flow control, path control, and many other network features. SNA provides these and much more, making it a very sophisticated technology with the capability of providing additional functionality at incremental expansions.

Probably the two most glaring differences between DEC networking products and IBM SNA products is one DEC strength and one IBM strength. The DEC strength is that Digital provides connectivity to a wide variety of technologies and to a wide variety of processor architectures; SNA is fairly limited in scope and capabilities and requires much manual intervention. The IBM strength is that the SNA product set provides very powerful network management tools (such as Network Communications Control Facility — NCCF, Network Problem Determination Application — NPDA, etc.), performance analyzers (VTAM Performance Analysis and Reporting System — VTAMPARS), cryptographic facilities, processing management, change management, and other features; DEC has few and they are marginally useful in many situations.

SNA Directions

What will IBM do with SNA and why do you care? Well, the general consensus in the networking world is that after the dust settles, there will be two main networking architectures: OSI and SNA. SNA is currently undergoing changes and IBM is also heavily involved in the OSI space as well (mostly to satisfy European customers who require OSI in their networks), so expect to see IBM continue to push SNA and, when available on IBM systems, OSI. Also, since IBM has to provide services to its customers, such as banks, and those customers will want to provide services on the Integrated Services Digital Network (ISDN) such as bank at home, shop at home, etc., for IBM to maintain market leverage in the mainframe area, it will have to provide ISDN connectivity, and ISDN connectivity means OSI communications capability.

Another main reason to watch SNA is IBM's push into the office automation space. IBM issues things called "Statements of Direction" that are essential to pay heed to if you are planning on keeping up with developments at IBM. In the area of office automation, the statement was made that "All IBM Office Systems Will Be Integrated." This is a fairly strong statement that has communications implications galore. With IBM's Distributed Office Support System (DISOSS) product set, the use of communications between systems is critical and getting more attention. When consideration is also given to two document standards on the market — DIA (Document Interchange Architecture: a method by which document formats, protocols, etc., are defined to communicate between end-users) and DCA (Document Content Architecture: a document representation methodology) — the fact that PU2.1 was recently created with the need of connecting items such as the Displaywriter and the Scanmaster 1 to an SNA network and the fact that IBM firmly recognizes the need to provide multifunction support in the office means that SNA will have to expand in scope and usage and will eventually become a favored method to connect office environments of IBM customers.

Another major reason for SNA watching is the IBM Systems Network Interconnect program (SNI). SNI provides for interconnection, protocol conversion, and gateways to other architectures and systems. While SNI is still somewhat new, it bears watching. IBM is like a large dragon. You can call it names, throw rocks, and poke at it until it decides to move. When it does decide to move, however, look out!

Chapter Summary

SNA is basically a hierarchical network with the ability to interconnect different types of actual hardware technologies, similar to other types of network architectures. Where SNA differs is in the wealth of connectivity offerings as well as the ability to support a great many integrated network management and connectivity tools. As such, it is a powerful and flexible architecture that provides configured networks with a plethora of network solutions to various business and scientific problems.

Chapter Ten

Transmission Control Protocol/Internet Protocol (TCP/IP)

INTRODUCTION

One of the problems with networks that is prevalent today is that there are many different protocols and network types. The hardware choices are confusing enough, but software protocol suites that run over the various types of network hardware solutions can absolutely boggle the mind. Ethernet, for instance, boasts a vast number of protocol suites such as DDCMP, LAT, MOP, XNS, SCS, TCP/IP, VRP, NRP, and a slew of other three-letter acronyms for various protocols that will solve all the problems a customer could have.

Within the scheme of protocols, however, some still seem to rear their ugly heads, no matter how hard the industry tries to put them down or get rid of them. One suite, Transmission Control Protocol/Internet Protocol, is such an occurrence. Every other vendor of networks will claim that their protocol is better and that TCP/IP is going away. Some will point to the decisions made by the Department of Defense to eventually migrate to internationally recognized and standardized communications hardware and protocols, obviating the need for TCP/IP and eventually replacing it. Some view TCP/IP as a workhorse whose time has come to be put out to pasture.

Then there are the zealots — those that think that the ONLY communications protocol suite for use in the world is TCP/IP and all others are fluff. These folks are dangerous because they not only are vocal about TCP/IP, many times they are UNIX zealots as well. Not that I have anything against UNIX or TCP, mind you. The problem is I have attended USENIX conferences before, so I know the truth about UNIX people.

Somewhere in the middle of the two camps are those who don't know what to do with TCP/IP or, worse, don't even really understand its significance to networks. Unfortunately, these individuals are usually the managers of such diverse camps of attitudes and must make decisions on whether to use TCP/IP on a project or not.

In this chapter, we will examine the TCP and IP networking protocols and some implementations that have become de-facto standards in the military area as well as academic and UNIX areas.

Some Explanation

Transmission Control Protocol (TCP) and Internet Protocol (IP) came about due to the various networking needs of the government. TCP/IP was developed to satisfy the need to interconnect various projects that included computer networks and also allow for the addition of dissimilar machines to the networks in a systematic, standardized manner. While it is quite true that smaller defense projects may not have warranted the use of TCP/IP for project aspects, edicts from various DOD concerns such, as the Undersecretary of Defense for Research and Development forced many government contractors and in-house developed projects to use the suite to conform with DOD requirements.

It's Not What Everybody Thinks It Is...

The TCP/IP suite is not a single protocol. Rather, it is a four-layer communications architecture that provides some reasonable network features, such as end-to-end communications, unreliable communications line fault handling, packet sequencing, internetwork routing, and specialized functions unique to DOD communications needs such as standardized message priorities. The bottom layer, network services, provides for communication to network hardware. Network hardware used in the various networks throughout the DOD typically reflects the usage of FIPS (Federal Information Processing Standard) compliant network hardware (such as IEEE 802 series of LANs and other technologies such as X.25). The layer above the network services layer is referred to as the internet protocol (IP) layer. The IP layer is responsible for providing a datagram service that routes data packets between dissimilar network architectures (such as between Ethernet and, say, X.25). IP has a few interesting qualities, one of which is the issue of data reliability. As a datagram service, IP does not guarantee delivery of data. Basically, if the data gets there, great. If not, that's OK too. Data concurrency, sequencing, and delivery guarantee is the job of the TCP protocol. TCP provides for error control, retransmission, packet sequencing, and many other capabilities. It is very complex and provides most of the features of the connection to other applications on other systems.

To understand properly what TCP/IP is all about, it is important to understand that: a) it is not OSI in implementation (although some argue that there are substantial similarities) and b) it is a unique network architecture that provides what are considered traditional network services in a manner that can be overhead intensive in some implementations.

How It Works

Most networks provide some sort of connection mechanism to get from point A to point B. Other networks worry about how to get from node A on network X to node B on network Y. If a program wishes to send information from itself on node A to another node on the same network, TCP will provide the packet sequencing, error control, and other services that are required to allow reliable end-to-end communications. This does not mean that IP is required. In fact, some implementations of TCP connect directly to the network services layer and bypass IP altogether. If, however, a program on node A on an Ethernet wished to connect to a destination program on node B on an X.25 network, an internet routing function would be necessary to get data packets sent properly between the two dissimilar network services. IP would take the packet from TCP, pass it

159

through a gateway that would provide conversion services, and then send the packet to the IP layer at the remote node for delivery to the remote TCP layer and, subsequently, the destination program. A good comparison would be as follows:

a) Program A on node ALPHA wishes to connect to program B on node BETA on the same network. Program A would send a data packet to TCP with the proper destination address. TCP would then encapsulate the data with the proper header and checksums in accordance with whatever services the program requested and pass the TCP packet to the IP layer. IP would then determine, from network directory information, that the remote node is on the same network as itself and simply pass the packet through to the network services layer for local network routing and delivery.

b) Program A on node ALPHA on network X wishes to connect to program B on node BETA on network Y. In this situation, data would be handled as in case a) above, but IP would determine that the destination is not on the local network. As a result, the IP layer in node ALPHA would determine the best route to get to the remote node and send the TCP packet to the next IP node in the path to get to the remote. IP does not care which program the source wants to connect to; all it cares about is which node to send the packets to.

IP nodes in the path from node ALPHA to node BETA will examine the packet to determine the destination and will forward the packet to the proper IP until it reaches the destination network IP. That IP determines that the node is on its local network and the packet is handed to the network services layer for the network on which BETA resides for delivery to node BETA.

Once the packet is received at the final destination IP, it is passed up to the TCP layer, which breaks out the packet header to figure out which program on the destination node is to receive the data. First, however, the packet header is examined carefully to insure that it has arrived in the proper sequence and that there are no special handling issues that need to be serviced. Once TCP is satisfied that everything is reasonable, the data is delivered to the destination program.

While all of this seems pretty straightforward, there are some implementation issues that make all of this complex. Since TCP and IP allow many service options such as message priority, security classification, data segmentation at the TCP level, packet segmentation at the IP level, and other issues that some network architectures, such as DECnet, need not concern themselves with, there can be some considerable overhead associated with packet processing. As a result, TCP/IP performance varies significantly from network hardware to network hardware as well as from machine implementation to machine implementation.

Now that we have examined the generalized delivery model, let's look at some of the specifics.

What TCP Was Built To Do

One of the base problems that TCP was built to address is the issue of connection from a particular program on a particular node on a particular network to a remote program destination that may or may not be on the same network as the originator. As such, a method of addressing nodes needed to be developed that identified a particular program on a particular node in a particular network. A possible solution is to develop hard addresses for all entities on a particular network. While this solves the problem, it is inflexible and usually does not provide an upwardly-flexible network architecture. Another problem is that some networks have their own proprietary (and sometimes bizarre) addressing scheme that must be considered as TCP/IP are above the local network addressing scheme mechanisms in the network architecture and will need to use the local mechanism on packet delivery. To solve the problem, TCP/IP uses a three-layer addressing mechanism that allows for delivery of packets across dissimilar network architectures.

161

To begin with, each program (called a PROCESS in TCP) has a unique one-up address on each machine. That unique local program address is combined with a particular node address to form something called a port. The port address is further combined with the local network address, forming a new entity called a socket. There can be many, many sockets on a TCP/IP network but each socket identifies, exactly, one specific application on a specific node on a specific network. Through this mechanism, IP will get the packets to the proper node and TCP will deliver the packet to the proper program on that node. Some nodes provide a standard process type (such as type 23 for remote log-ins) that are "known" to other network entities and that provide certain standard services. Through this mechanism, TCP provides a multiplexing capability that is essential in the efficient use of the network resource.

From One Socket to Another

As with any network, two sockets that wish to connect to each other must have a mechanism by which this happens. TCP provides this in various ways. One of the more common ways connections are established is via an ACTIVE/PASSIVE network OPEN. A PASSIVE OPEN is when a receptive socket declares itself to be open and available for incoming connections (this would typically be the mode used by something like a database server). A PASSIVE OPEN, however, may be set up in various ways. First, the PASSIVE OPEN may be set up to be FULLY SPECIFIED, which means that the socket issuing the PASSIVE OPEN tells the network exactly which socket may connect to it, including security levels allowed and other related details. Another type of PASSIVE OPEN is the UNSPECIFIED PASSIVE OPEN in which the socket will accept any connection request from any remote socket provided that the remote system requesting connection meets prescribed security and other criteria. In both types of network OPENs, it is pertinent to point out that the socket OPENing the network may also declare timeout values for all data received from the originator of the connection. This allows for the expeditious handling of data as well as providing a means by which "old" messages are handled in a reasonable fashion and messages requiring special handling (in terms of time) are processed correctly.

Another type of OPEN is the ACTIVE OPEN. Unlike the PASSIVE OPEN, the ACTIVE OPEN aggressively seeks a connection to a particular socket. An ACTIVE OPEN will only be successful if there is a cooperating and corresponding PASSIVE OPEN or other ACTIVE OPEN from the destination socket.

Once a connection has been established between two sockets, data may be transferred between the sockets. TCP provides several mechanisms for data transfer, but the two most popular are segmented data transfer and PUSH mode. Segmented data transfer allows TCP to send user data in chunks across the network. As such, TCP may send the data in such a manner that allows for the best efficiency for the network being used. This means that even if the user has transferred 25 blocks of user data to TCP, TCP may not send it all at once, opting to segment the data in such a manner as to provide optimal flow of data on the network. While this technique is great for data flow issues and network congestion issues, it can be troublesome for transfers in which the data needs to get to the remote system NOW! In such cases, the user may specify the PUSH flag. A PUSH request forces TCP to send whatever has been passed from the user to TCP right away with no consideration for optimal flow control. In addition to the PUSH flag, the user may specify the urgency of the data being transferred to keep the remote system on its toes.

How much data is allowed to be sent from one socket to another is a function of the network and programs involved. Since TCP was developed with multiple network architectures in mind, it allows some level of link negotiation on connection and data transfer that provides for maximum buffer sizes (somewhat dynamically) and maximum buffer allocation.

TCP Sequencing

To insure that everything gets to where it is going and in the proper order, TCP provides packet sequencing services as well as error detection

163

functions utilizing a 16-bit checksum in the TCP header area. It is also interesting to note that TCP presumes the IP layer to be unreliable and, therefore, includes a 96-bit pseudoheader in front of the actual TCP packet header that includes the source address, destination address, protocol being used, and segment size. Through the use of the pseudoheader, TCP protects itself from IP delivering the packet to the wrong place (or not at all) by misinterpreting TCP header fields. The checksum in the TCP header also includes the pseudoheader bits to insure that everything is clean when it hits the remote side.

After the connection is established and all data has been transferred, the link may be shut down via user request. This is the clean way. It is very possible that the link may also be abruptly aborted due to link drop or some catastrophic failure of the network or socket-to-socket linkage. TCP provides mechanisms to handle both situations. A CLOSE primitive issuance tells TCP that the user is finished with the network link and to close down the link gracefully by sending all remaining data in local buffers and notifying the remote socket that the sending user wishes to CLOSE the link. The remote TCP socket notifies the user that a CLOSE has been issued. The user may then send any remaining data and issue a CLOSE to the sender. When the sender receives the CLOSE acknowledgment from the receiver, it sends a TERMINATE to the user and notifies the remote TCP that a TERMINATE has been issued. The remote TCP socket sends a TERMINATE to the remote user and the link is closed completely.

If a network link abort occurs, for whatever reason, the ABORT primitive is sent to the remote TCP, which tells the remote user that a TERMINATE has occurred. No more data of any kind is transmitted on the link and the link is closed immediately on both sides. Obviously, a link termination of the ABORT kind is not desirable, as data may be lost and other integrity issues may be involved.

TCP Needs Not an IP

It is important to understand that TCP need not be connected to an IP, although that is frequently the case. TCP provides the essential network connection and data transfer features a user would require to connect with a particular program on a remote system. Some companies use TCP as the protocol of choice when setting up simple direct-connect network connections (where the remote node is hard-wired to the originating node) or when performing tasks such as downline system loading. In any case, TCP is a powerful and full-featured protocol that provides reasonable network services for user data.

Many times, however, just getting the data from one socket to another may involve the connection to various types of network technologies. A TCP packet coming in from an asynchronous link may need to be routed on to an Ethernet to reach its ultimate destination. Because of the need to connect and properly route data through to its proper network and destination socket, the IP layer was developed.

What's an IP?

Internet Protocol (IP) is a datagram service. It basically provides rudimentary internetwork routing services without any regard to the destination program, TCP formats, error control, packet sequencing, etc. Its function in life is to get the packet to the right network and, eventually, to the right node. Further, IP allows for expedited routing of packets that need to get to a destination quicker than other, routine packets. In many respects, with the exception of routing priority, IP functionality is similar to Ethernet packet handling. If a packet arrives that is damaged (there is an IP checksum), the packet is discarded. What is in the data field of the packet is of no interest to IP. IP could be sending a TCP packet or some other protocol for all it cares. As long as the proper SEND (user sending to the network) primitive fields have been filled in, IP will send the packet on its merry way. When the packet reaches the remote node and the checksum figures out OK, IP sends the packet to TCP (or whatever the receptor protocol is) via a DELIVER directive and all is well with the universe. If the packet gets trashed in the process of being delivered, so be it. If the packets arrive out of sequence, that's not IP's problem. If a packet is missing, again, IP does not care. IP gets the data packet (usually a TCP packet) from point A on network X to point B on network Y. That's all, nothing more.

Gateways and IP

To provide the internetwork routing function, IP makes use of special nodes called gateways. A gateway, in IP terms, is a machine that allows two dissimilar networks to be connected to each other. The two networks may or may not be the same type (Ethernet, X.25, token ring, etc.), as IP operates above the hardware itself and is only interested in the virtual connection function, not the physical path or hardware used. As such, there may be a need to segment large messages from the upper software layers into sizes that are applicable to the remote network's allowances. To do this, IP will segment large messages into proper-sized chunks (such as when going from 1500 byte Ethernet packets to 128 byte X.25 packets) for the destination network and reassemble them at the remote destination IP layer before delivery to the user. If a packet gets destroyed in the segmented message and the remote IP detects the packet loss, the entire segment is killed off by the remote IP. Obviously, TCP would detect that a segment is missing and request a retransmission from the remote TCP for any missing packets. TCP has the option of forcing IP NOT to segment packets, but this is usually not implemented as it can cause routing problems where differing network technologies are concerned.

IP also provides for proper security classification of packets being sent to a remote site. If an intermediary gateway or network is not at least the same security level as the transmitted packet, the packet will not be sent through that network. As a result, some strange routing of data may occur sometimes as IP must contend with the problem of expeditious routing but also the problem of security-oriented routing.

Finally, IP has some different terminology than that typically used in a network. In many networks, the concept of a "hop" is the routing of a data packet through a node on its way to its final destination point. In IP, a hop is when a data packet goes through a gateway to another network. Therefore, it is quite possible that a packet may wander through various nodes in a local network before it actually gets to the remote network gateway, depending, of course, upon previously discussed variables. If the packet does not incur a route through a gateway, it, in IP terms, has not incurred a hop. If it transverses through two gateways, it would be considered to have incurred two hops on its path to the final destination. Hops, therefore, are not referred to in the same manner as many other popular communications architectures.

As can be seen, TCP and IP are not the same and may actually be implemented totally independent of each other for separate uses. More often than not, however, they are both included in many offerings from various vendors.

TCP/IP Applications

In any network architecture, the protocols and transmission methods are not enough. Users frequently want and need utilities that implement the protocols in the network architecture to allow file transfer, program communication, virtual terminal support, and electronic mail. Most TCP/IP implementations are the same and a few standard applications exist.

File Transfer

First off, file transfer facilities are usually provided for by a mechanism known as the File Transfer Protocol (FTP). FTP is a simple featured file-moving utility that allows a record-oriented (one record at a time) transfer, a block transfer (which moves chunks of a file), or an image transfer (which does not look in any way at the file contents). Further, FTP knows about EBCDIC and ASCII (also NVT-ASCII) and may provide some rudimentary conversion facilities BEFORE a transfer begins. As file

167

systems are very complex and the need for file transfer between systems is growing, FTP has evolved in some cases to special implementations that know how to convert specific file formats between certain types of machine architectures. This conversion facility is not within the defined scope of FTP, but some vendors include the conversion features anyway. To transfer a file, the user invokes the host FTP utility, specifies file name, type (if necessary), remote destination, and off it goes. One interesting feature on some FTP implementations is the recovery facility. Networks, as most are well aware, will fail from time to time. In the case of failure, any transfers in process will usually have to be restarted from scratch. If the file is being transferred with FTP in block mode, it may be possible to resume the transfer at a later time by specifying which block was the last transmitted. FTP would then continue to send the file as if nothing had happened. This feature is not available on all FTP implementations and has some host and remote system software considerations involved with it, but, all in all, it is a useful feature to have when transferring very large files.

Terminal Connectivity in a Virtual Way

Another popular utility is one known as TELNET. TELNET is a virtual terminal facility that allows a user to connect to a remote system as if the user's terminal were hard-wired to that remote system. As with file systems, virtual terminals may need to emulate a wide variety of terminals, which may be impractical on larger, complex networks. As such, TELNET provides a basic protocol handling facility and a negotiation facility that allows for the inclusion of different types of terminal protocols and signaling mechanisms.

It's in the Mail

A final utility that is somewhat popular is the Simple Mail Transfer Protocol or SMTP as it is more affectionately known. SMTP provides a mechanism by which a user can specify a destination address (or addresses if to more than one remote user), a particular path to follow (if desired), and a message. Like other electronic mail systems, SMTP provides for return receipts, forwarding of mail, and other similar features. The only odd issue has to do with the problem of the term "simple." Having used SMTP for some years now, it is not intuitive and the routing issues can get strange. Yet, it is a useful utility and heavily used in the defense area.

Whose Implementation Is Best?

Some vendors of TCP/IP have made a cozy living out of providing their wares to defense contractors and UNIX/Ultrix shops that need to connect and communicate with their compatriots supporting TCP/IP. How the vendors have implemented TCP and IP varies greatly, which also means that features and performance vary significantly. Some vendors, such as Excelan, have chosen to implement much of the protocol suite in a controller card, effectively offloading the host from the duties of running TCP and IP programs and utilities and yet providing the necessary connectivity. This is nice as it offloads the host and makes the overall system more cost effective and less bogged down in the network mire. Other companies, such as Wollongong, have chosen to implement TCP/IP in software on the host. This degrades the host system, sometimes severely, but has the advantage of being able to function as a true IP node, allowing connection to various network technologies simultaneously.

Each implementation has its benefits and drawbacks. Which one is best for a particular system depends heavily upon cost factors, system loading expectations, and how many different kinds of networks a site may be connected to. Some vendors have begun to introduce TCP/IP routers that allow IP services to different types of networks by connecting the networks through a dedicated IP router (sometimes referred to as an IMP) and allowing TCP messages to be created by a particular network protocol, translated into TCP and sent to a destination node. The source node thinks that it is talking to a machine running the same protocol on the same network. In reality, the packet has been translated and set to the destination node on either the same or another network. Such routing and translation trickery is beginning to become more and more prevalent in environments where TCP and other types of networking software exist.

In the quest to TCP/IP or not TCP/IP, the bottom line is how long can it last? A few years ago I would have said that it was a safe bet that usage of TCP/IP would last a company for some years to come. Now that the Department of Defense will, in the future, no longer require the absolute use of TCP/IP, opting, instead, to go with OSI, such is not a safe bet for all sites. There are enough TCP sites installed that it would be foolish and expensive to haul off and convert all sites to something else. It is also prudent to remember that the number of networked machines that will appear by 1995 will far eclipse anything currently installed in such a way as to make protocols such as TCP/IP become a minority. Much has to do with who is buying what as to how long it will last. I would venture a guess, however, and bet that TCP/IP will be around for a while, if to do nothing else than support current systems. As those systems cut over to OSI, however, fewer and fewer nodes will be seen running TCP or IP in favor of OSI.

What would I do if I had to buy today? Buy TCP/IP, of course. Why? Because it works and it is now. It would serve very nicely for the short term (2-4 years) and give the OSI packages some time to mature before diving in headlong. A nice side benefit is that the OSI transport service and TCP's capabilities are very similar, as are the OSI network layer routing service and the IP services. Further, TCP/IP prescribes standardized network hardware, so OSI-compliant hardware is a given in many TCP/IP environments, allowing a nice migration path to OSI at a future date. If one installs OSI-compliant hardware, then conversion to OSI from TCP/IP is not as traumatic as it could be.

Chapter Comments

TCP/IP is a serious protocol suite. It provides reasonable network services for most applications and is extensible, well documented, and fairly straightforward to implement. Best, it is capable of connecting dissimilar machines on dissimilar networks together into one big happy network. After all, that's all we really want anyway, isn't it?

Chapter Eleven

Network Encryption

INTRODUCTION

There's a lot of concern these days over the issue of network intrusions. Any reputable network manager KNOWS that there is some hacker out there somewhere trying to bust into his or her network and get at all those goodies that are on his or her systems. And for you network managers who are not paranoid about the security on your network, remember the old adage about paranoia: "Just because you are not paranoid does not mean that someone is not out to get you."

Obviously, network security is more than making sure the network passwords are known only to the chosen few. Network security is usually thought of as a multilayered management chore consisting of technical actions, management actions, and user training. But, this chapter is not about all the necessary precautions for a truly secure network. This chapter looks at network encryption techniques, what they are, how they work, and why you would want to use network encryption on your network.

Encryption systems always conjure up the image of James Bond (007 — not encrypted) or some guy trying to get the Nazi codebook with all the German encryption codes for the rest of the war off of the U-boat (which is, naturally, 300 feet under water) headed for Italy, without, of course, being noticed or caught. In other words, Hollywood has managed to give encryption systems a certain mystique associated with clandestine activities, beautiful women, exotic places, and ACTION.

Imagine my disappointment when I got my Data Encryption Standard (DES) network encryption box and found it to be about the size of a shoebox, white (not black), and fully documented including a complete explanation of the algorithm used and how to set up your own codes. How depressing! I had at least expected a Junior Space Cadet decoder ring and was hoping for an envelope with "Destroy Immediately After Reading" on it.

The reality of encryption is that it is not magical, mystical, or even exciting. Encryption simply involves the usage of an encipherment algorithm with a key (like a password) to take normal network data and scramble it into bits that only a system with the encryption algorithm and the proper key can understand. The problem is that most people tend to look at encryption in the mystical sense and few understand what it really is.

To facilitate the use of encryption by the public sector, the National Bureau of Standards (NBS) published a Federal Information Processing Standard (FIPS PUB 46) on January 15, 1977, called the Data Encryption Standard (DES). The DES uses a 64-bit key structure implemented with a defined permutation (change mechanism) method. Fifty six bits are used for the actual key and 8 bits are used for error control. If you compute out the various combinations of a 56-bit key, you will find that there are over 70 quatrillion different bit combinations; the chances of breaking a properly enciphered DES data stream are pretty slim unless, of course, someone has access to the key that is being used. With the DES, data is enciphered in 64-bit blocks.

Encrypting a data packet with DES is a stepwise procedure. First, the 64-bit block worth of data undergoes a permutation that arranges the data according to a specific matrix. The 64-bit block is split into two halves (32-bits each) and the right half is permuted to a 48-bit value (the matrix that specifies the order of data happens to duplicate 16 bits of the data). The generated 48-bit value is the exclusive-ORed with a 48-bit key value that is obtained from the original 56-bit DES key. The exclusive-OR operation reduces the 48-bit value to a 32-bit by splitting up the 48-bit value to eight groups of 6 bits. The 6-bit values are then converted to 4-bit values using a 6-bit to 4-bit selection table. Following the conversion of

174

the 48-bit data to 32-bit data, the 32-bit data is permuted again to a new 32-bit value. Now, if this were not complicated enough, when the data on the right is reduced to 32-bits, this value is exclusive-ORed to the unaltered left 32-bits. This completes the first level of iteration of the encryption computation.

The result generated from the previous computation now becomes the right half and the unaltered right half becomes the left half. The data then is permuted 16 different times in a specific fashion, only using 16 different keys (one new key per permutation). Following the 16 permutations, the data is permuted one last time, only in the reverse order that it was permuted in the very first time. The data is now encrypted and ready for transmission.

My reaction the first time I walked through the standard years ago was that I could achieve the same effect by allowing a lot of noise on the line, but the people at NBS didn't think it was funny. The government doesn't have a great sense of humor.

It is important to note that DES has been implemented in a wide variety of products other than networking and communications products. File encryption, password encryption, and other traditional computing components have been given the benefit of the DES encryption algorithm to secure access to sensitive system components.

Another encryption method that is gaining some notoriety is a mechanism known as the RSA (for Rivest-Shamir-Adelman) Public Key Scheme. The RSA scheme is simple, yet very secure. The idea revolves around the fact that it is much easier to multiply prime numbers together than it is to factor the result. This means that the result could be used as part of the encyphering key, yet not compromise the necessary factors required for the decyphering operation. If the result generated were, say, over 100 digits long, it would take billions of years to factor out the result on a high-speed computer using the best algorithms possible. All in all, it is an elegant, high-speed method to encrypt data and keep it secure. An example of how to encrypt/decrypt data with the RSA mechanism is in figure 2. For you folks using X.25 communications, you should be aware that the RSA algorithm is being pushed for usage as the authentication mechanism for the X.32 subset.

Everyone has their own opinions on the following and I am no different, so I'm sure I'm going to draw a few comments on this topic. That's good, though, 'cause my Dad always used to say that unless someone disagrees with you, no one is thinking (he used to have other sayings, too, but none that I think would be acceptable for printing). So, now that we have seen how a couple of the major public encryption mechanisms work, by now you are wondering to yourself as to where you might implement encryption in a network?

Actually, encryption could be implemented anywhere in the network architecture, but the fastest way is within the communications hardware. This is further justified when one considers that DES is already on a chip (the Motorola MC6859, the Burroughs MC884, Western Digital WD2001E/F, WD2002A/B, and WD2003, Advanced Micro Devices AmZ8068, Intel 8294, TI TMS9940, American Microsystems\S6894 and other multichip sets and board products) and the RSA mechanism is math-computation intensive (making it ideal for something like an 8087 arithmetic coprocessor or other such chips). But, while encryption at the communications interface level is the simplest, it does not keep the node secure. From a system management point of view, encryption of data BEFORE it hits the network architecture is usually preferable as it precludes network software and hardware from performing data encryption. Should the network be compromised, the data is already encrypted on the node. It is also reasonable to perform encryption at the session control layer (and below) of the network architecture; this insures that outgoing data is secure before it hits the network communications hardware. While this sounds good on paper, it can also cause a great deal of computational overhead due to encryption of seemingly innocuous transactions such as ACKs and NACKs as well as other problems such as when to encrypt data and when not to (such as in the case of downline loading).

Encryption of data prior to hitting the network architecture or encryption in the hardware precludes the network software from having to make all kinds of decisions about when and where to encrypt data.

Finally, the big question: Why bother with network encryption?

Besides the obvious answer of keeping the IBM users out of your DECnet network, there are some very good reasons. First off, the old adage "An ounce of prevention is worth a pound of cure" definitely applies to networks. In areas where line tapping is possible, the cost of implementing network encryption equipment can be far less than the loss of data or market edge caused by network intrusion. Line tapping involves more than someone tapping a telephone connection. Line tapping is the term also used on public data networks when a node on the network intercepts an in-progress communications session. It is also useful to get a bit paranoid about local area networks (LANs), especially nonintrusively tapped networks (such as Ethernet), as nodes could easily be added and the network software may not necessarily pick up the new node as a node on the network (this is common on networks that support different protocols). Software encryption in the network architecture prevents "session" tapping by nodes. For instance, node A could be establishing a connection to node B, but a different node X makes A think that it is node B. By the use of a network encryption algorithm, X would HAVE to know the encryption key, which is highly unlikely, to simulate node B.

Encryption, strategically placed within the node, can be a very useful thing to have. Many is the time that embarrassing moments have happened at many companies due to unauthorized users reading files or electronic mail messages. Through the use of encryption techniques, such encounters become rare, if at all, and business relationships can be salvaged. Encryption can take place at the file level, file system level, or even at the image level. Some companies have programs available that allow the encryption of executable images such that a key has to be supplied for the image to run. While this may be somewhat troublesome, it does keep circumvention of the normal system protection mechanisms to a minimum and allows control over who has the key(s).

One thing to keep in mind in the implementation of encryption systems is the problem of access to the encryption mechanism. If the mechanism used is hardware, it is important that the component(s) be kept in a manner where it can be physically secure from tampering and, if tampered with, leaves some sort of notification that tampering has happened. If the method used involves software encryption, it becomes much more difficult to keep tampering from happening. But, just as with monitoring hardware tampering, it is critical that some sort of mechanism be placed in the encryption software to keep tampering from happening.

Encryption of data in networks will become a necessity in the modern corporate environment as a matter of course. How you decide to implement encryption in your corporate environment will have a lot to do with what tradeoffs in performance you can live with. In all cases, it would be a good thing to start to look into. Who knows? Your network may be the next "statistic."

Chapter Twelve

Office Automation Networks

INTRODUCTION

Ham and eggs. Death and taxes. Politics and corruption. Nixon and Memorex. A Coke (Classic, not the fake stuff) and a smile.

Some things just go together.

Office automation and networks.

Sure, you say. More like mixing oil and water.

Not true, mon frere. Networks do go well with office automation. As a matter of fact, office automation is ripe for networks. Send files over to another system. Send a mail message to a remote node. Share calendar files between networks. Without a network, such occurrences would be rare and difficult.

Basic Issues

Before we get too carried away, let's look at some sample statistics about offices:

a) Office consists of space, people, office-specific functions, office-specific equipment, and traffic
b) 90% of all offices have under 30 users
   8% of all offices have 30-300 users
   2% of all offices have over 300 but under 3000 users
c) An average office has about 115 users

d) An average total office size is about 175'x175'
e) Individual offices average 10'x10'
f) Offices change regularly (people, organization, equipment, work load, etc.)
g) Offices usually need specific services geared for offices:
  1) Basic support (calendar management, office directories, personnel records, schedules, basic computation)
  2) Text/word processing (correspondence, forms, mailings, data entry, message review)
  3) Data processing (advanced computational capabilities, file manipulation and access, graphic formats, heavy printing)
  4) Management information (database access (internal/external), program support (DSS), operations planning and monitoring)
  5) Electronic mail (send, receive, edit, forward, etc.)
  6) Record management (indexing, filing, and retrieving internally and externally delivered documents)
h) Office traffic tends to be "bursty" (sporadic) in nature, with most network traffic averaging 1-100 bytes
i) Response time is essential for some office applications, especially in client services areas

As can be seen, offices are not like other types of computational environments like real time acquisition systems, factory automation, numerical control, scientific programming, or even specific commercial types of application programming. Office automation is a science unto itself, one that requires the occasional mad scientist-type to figure out what to do to solve complex office problems.

Office networks used for office automation require that the standard network planning cycle be considered and implemented. In addition to that, however, there are some other considerations that may need to be thought about if networks and office products are to work well together:

a) What kind of office products will be connected together?
b) What is the expected increase of users and services offered?

c) How many different types of formats will be used in internal file organization?

d) Will dissimilar vendor machines be used to provide office services?

e) What kind of communications media is being considered for connection to office computing and support equipment (such as printers, smart copiers, graphics plotting systems, fax machines, etc.)

f) What kind of electronic mail systems will be supported?

g) Has there been consideration for future office issues with networks such as ISDN and FDDI interconnects?

While this is obviously an incomplete list, it is provided to induce some thought processes and get you thinking about networks and office automation (OA).

Office Network Technologies

Office networks of the 80s are not at all like any other time in the history of the office. Much of this is due to the introduction of the Ethernet technology in the late 70s and early 80s by Xerox. Xerox, a company vitally interested in automating the office place, developed Ethernet with the intent of using it in the office environment. Early drawings of Ethernet configurations show corporate systems, departmental systems, disks, printers, optical storage systems, filing systems, facsimile systems, copiers/printers and a host of other office products all on the same network segment. Some of this has reached the age of truth: systems, printers, disks, and other types of peripherals have slowly but very surely been popping up on Ethernets and finding happy homes in office networks around the world. But, many say, this is the tip of the iceberg.

Oh yeah? What's next?

Voice on Ethernet. Yes, PBX communications and voice support. Faster, fiber-based Ethernets capable of not 10 or 50 or 100 megabits/second (Mbps), but Ethernets over 100 mega-BYTES (MB/sec). Image

181

processing subsystems tied together via Ethernet. Optical storage subsystems allowing global storage and retrieval over Ethernet. Still video (frame) over Ethernet that allows incremental animation technologies and video-oriented databases, etc. In short, Ethernet technology is not just a coax cable anymore; it is a flexible, migration-oriented technology that will allow usage of the technology in places where it has not previously been considered.

Ethernet implementations besides fiber are being introduced now. The venerable twisted pair technology, much used and much maligned, is making a comeback. AT&T has developed a technique for wiring office environments using twisted pair technology it calls the Premesis Distribution System (PDS). PDS is a hub-based, twisted pair topology that allows transmission of data and/or voice over networks that are simple to connect and configure that are flexible enough for the office environment but powerful enough to handle the data volumes modern offices require. While PDS is supposed to be "transmission technology independent," AT&T designed PDS with its StarLAN product in mind. StarLAN, a 1Mbps network, provides Ethernet like connectivity with the flexibility of twisted pair. By supporting a slower transmission speed on the twisted pair network, AT&T effectively allows a flexible and noise-tolerant network configuration while allowing a reasonable number of connections to be included, all at a reasonable price. Not to be caught short by AT&T, other companies have jumped on the PDS bandwagon and are offering PDS-compatible and certified (meaning AT&T has checked the network technology to insure that it will work on PDS wiring topologies that are installed in the prescribed PDS manner). However, 1Mbps speed is not enough for some vendors. Companies such as 3Com are offering PDS-certified twisted pair Ethernets that run at 10Mbps, just like the baseband coax implementation. Such network offerings, while substantially faster than the 1Mbps StarLAN, have some configuration issues that cause problems. First, the few twisted pair Ethernets that have been introduced to the marketplace have shown a great resistance to noise and other office-common interference problems. Second, twisted pair Ethernets that run at the 10Mbps speed provide such speed for only short stretches of cable such as 70-100 meter lengths with a limited number of taps on the cable segments. To provide longer twisted pair Ethernets requires the use of many repeaters and bridges to allow the connectivity between many nodes. In a recent office cabling experience, my customer wanted a twisted pair Ethernet to be implemented to take advantage of the latest and greatest technology. We finally, after three weeks and several major problems, got part of the network running. It turns out that fast twisted pair technology is much more intolerant of connection rules, noise factors, and other interference issues than thinwire, thickwire, or broadband Ethernets.

Bottom line is this: twisted pair is here and coming along quickly. It makes sense for many applications, especially offices where there is probably already a ton of twisted pair run all over the place. It also makes sense because twisted pair is cheap, easy to run, and available everywhere. Running twisted pair for Ethernet, especially the current 10Mbps version run by different vendors, such as 3Com, DEC, and others, requires a little more care than standard twisted pair cable runs for terminals. In my recent experience, we found that seemingly innocuous office equipment such as ballasts on incandescent overhead lighting caused interference problems. Don't jump into twisted pair Ethernet just yet, but DO consider it for the office environment, as it is a reasonable way to go for office networks.

Why rattle on about Ethernet? It was built for the office. It was designed for short, bursty traffic and for a large number of connections. It was also designed to be adaptable and extensible on demand, as conditions in the office change.

Token Ring and the Office

Some office networks are built around token ring networks. The IBM Token Ring(IEEE 802.5) is the most popular ring so far, but this has been because the network is "IBM" and because IBM has finally started to ship the network to its customer base. Typically, IBM recommends the token ring in offices where a network is desired that requires connection to departmental computers and corporate (mainframe) resources. In other, smaller (less than 70 nodes) networks without such larger resources that are mostly IBM PC-oriented, IBM will sell the PC Network, but with reluctance. Why? Because it is basically a Sytek broadband Ethernet product that allows the PCs to connect and not an IBM-developed or globally blessed technology. Many IBM office products, however, are beginning to appear with token ring support built in or with the option to install token ring as a preferred technology (e.g., the PS/2) and a continual push into this area is expected with the enhancements to PROFS, DISOSS, and other office products such as copiers/printers and the like.

For those who can't make up their mind and decide to implement both 802.5 (token ring) and 802.3 (Ethernet), there is hope as well. As mentioned in previous articles, the Fiber Distributed Data Interface (FDDI) is moving nicely along. FDDI provides a high-speed (100Mbit per ring, dual ring) fiber-based network backbone that can be run over a distance of 200 kilometers (124 miles). A major purpose of FDDI is to provide connectivity between the IEEE 802 series of networks, effectively allowing, say, Ethernet nodes to converse, transparently, with token ring nodes. It is difficult, today, to accomplish such a feat. This is not going to last much longer. By incorporation of OSI architecture and protocols into software and the inclusion of FDDI between Ethernets and token ring networks, soon it won't matter much what kind of LAN was selected for the office: they will all connect anyway. Transparently.

Other office network technologies include demonstration networks that use infrared connections between office systems. Through this manner, cabling becomes a nonissue, but environment becomes a more important one. One major microcomputer vendor is even experimenting with the introduction of a keyboard and mouse system that uses infrared communications methods rather than cable. This type of communications technology is attractive in the office as offices are volatile places. Nothing ever stays in the same place in most offices and about the time that you think that they will, they change again. Now when office equipment and systems move around, the network "moves" as well without recabling.

Office Computing Systems

When looking at the office from a network point of view, one has to consider the types of systems that are typically in use in the office environment. Personal (although anymore I think that they should be called professional because there is nothing "personal" about them) computers are welcomed guests in many offices, with the IBM PC and PS being the most popular. Close behind and gaining is the Macintosh. These types of computer systems usually provide office workstations functions: word processing, spreadsheets, financial modeling tools, desktop publishing, and many other related functions. Of computing systems used in the office, they are also the most popular and have been pulling a lot of the weight in office computing. This, however, is starting to change.

Departmental Computing

Office computing is giving way to a new term that is starting to permeate the overall office automation marketplace: departmental computers. Through the use of departmental computing systems, department offices can provide group connectivity technology, mail, word processing, scheduling, and all the usual office functions but at a reasonable price and with demonstrable results. Using PCs in the workplace helps productivity, but the cost of providing each person his/her own PC is very prohibitive. Cheaper PC hardware doesn't solve the problems as software licensing still cost $$$s and management of resources on multiple PCs is still a hassle. Through the use of a departmental "hub" system, a functional department in a company can allow sharing of services and provision of office automation functions to more individuals at a reasonable cost.

Departmental computing has some computer vendors worried. Because departments basically "own" their own system, more and more system managers are individuals with no formal computer science training or background or with any experience in managing any type of computer. Further, these individuals may also be responsible for their own network realm (between the departmental system and connected PC systems) and applications, which further complicates a tough job. Departmental computing in the office also has some MIS departments worried, too. Now the "users" of the network and hub components are in charge of their "own" systems, causing MIS management headaches and serious political problems throughout a company.

Why the move to departmental computing? Cost of doing business with MIS departments ("it takes too long and is too expensive to get MIS to do anything for us"), a need to be "free from corporate control," greater autonomy in application decisions, and lower cost, powerful computers. The MicroVAX II and MicroVAX 2000 are good examples as to why departmental computing is a real craze these days. With a reasonable cost, a department gets autonomy and compute power. Also, since the Micro-VAX runs good 'ole VMS or Ultrix, migration to larger systems as applications get too large for the MicroVAX system is a breeze. To add fuel to the fire, support of DECnet connectivity and terminal services on Ethernet makes the MicroVAX departmental solution a very attractive one for many companies.

Frankly, the MicroVAX also has some vendors worried. I was talking to a friend at IBM recently and he said that one of their greatest concerns was departmental computing and LANs. Their second greatest concern was the MicroVAX. Why, I asked.

"Simple. The 9370 is too expensive for many departments and there are compatibility issues even between IBM operating systems. We also have the problem of network connectivity. The 9370 has Ethernet and capability for a token ring, but we only support TCP/IP at present and it is not known when SNA will be supported (or if) on IBM LANs," he responded.

Don't expect IBM to place all of its hopes in the 9370. The System 36 is a neat little system and is quite capable of providing office functions. It, too, can also talk to Ethernet very nicely and some third party companies have taken it upon themselves to develop compatibility packages for the System 36 that work like TCP/IP, DECnet, and other popular networking technologies. Even though I am a hard-core DEC user/programmer, I even have a System 36 because of some things that work better there than on the VAXes. It installs cleanly, networks nicely, and is easy to use and support.

Another issue with office systems and networks is the coming waves of mini-supercomputers. Right now we have super-minicomputers — 32-bit architectures with enough ka-zots to provide computing features for most standard, current office functions. In the near future, however, mini-supercomputers will be more popular and will allow parallel processing capabilities, image processing and interpretation, and other very compute-intensive functions that are not in offices today due to the need for major horsepower to run such tasks. With the advent of a "mini-Cray" architecture in a department, the capabilities of generating big-time data loads on systems and networks becomes a reality. Instead of simple graphics and plots, high-res graphics and still video become feasible and probable. Worse, users will want to connect these resources together and exchange high volumes of such data, a taxing task for a network to be sure. Storage to networked disks will be imperative, as will remote access from local machines and remotely networked machines.

Along the lines of mini-supercomputers and networks comes the issue of input into office systems. Right now, it is not uncommon for typing to be the main method of access. Optical character readers and scanning systems are starting to become popular with less and less expensive systems becoming more and more powerful and available to the general office community. Companies such as IBM, DEC, and Kurtzweil are experimenting with voice recognition systems that will allow nontypists (such as senior managers) to use computing hardware without the need to type in information. Further, for those of us who type slower than we talk, we can now send information, memos, and other documents we would normally not undertake easier than ever, as typing will become a secondary method of input. While this may not seem related to networks, it is.

Granted that networks handle a high volume of data in an office now. In the near future, networks will need to handle exponentially higher volumes of data due to the ease in which data can be inserted into a system. With voice commands to PCs and departmental computers, multiple commands may be tried in short order and faster response to such commands will be essential to satisfying user demands. Networks will need to rise to the challenge if the office of the future is to provide the needed user connectivity and services that many vendors expect to provide.

How far off is voice recognition? Some distance for continuous speech, but there are already some $5-10,000.00 word recognition packages that plug into PCs that have a respectable vocabulary and that can be useful in the office environment. In a few more years when computing hardware becomes powerful enough to handle the logic necessary for such operations, voice recognition and storage will become commonplace and necessary in the office.

Now that we have discussed some of the implementation and hardware issues, let's look at some of the software issues in office networks.

The Format Problem

One of the major problems with networks in the office is that of file formats and formats of interchangeable "items." What this means is that not all office system packages provide uniform, standardized formats for products, which makes the transfer and support of such products difficult from vendor to vendor.

Networks are lucky. Over time, standards have been developed that are allowing more and more networks to be connected in a reasonable manner that provides various types of connectivity. Because some of the networks are internationally standardized protocols and architectures, the implementation of networks in offices is becoming easier and easier, and the easing of migration headaches from architecture to architecture is starting to happen. Office packages, however, still generate files. And, to date, there is no standard internal file format mechanism for all types of files that are generated in the office environment. Sure, there are DIF and DCA, but what about graphics interchange standards and other issues such as image graphics interchange? Some are starting to appear, but still have a way to go.

Standards are just starting to hit office automation in the networking area. The X.400 standard, a messaging standard used frequently for electronic mail, is one of the most important standards to appear in a while for office automation. By adhering to the message transfer agent/user agent model proposed by the X.400 mail standard, noncompatible computer hardware and software architectures may exchange electronic mail messages between each other. Further, servers (message transfer agents or MTAs) may be developed that convert electronic mail messages from a particular vendor format to a format compliant with X.400 and send the message on its merry way across the network. In fact, this type of mechanism, called a mail router or X.400 mail gateway, has been developed by various vendors (including DEC) as a method to exchange mail messages between dissimilar machine and operating systems architectures.

But why is X.400 such a big deal in office networks? Oddly enough, the two main areas of interest in an office automation system are word processing and electronic mail. Secondary to those immediate interests are things like scheduling systems and spreadsheets. Therefore, the ability to exchange electronic mail between dissimilar machines is very important, as offices are often run by more than one type of system.

X.400 is more than "just" X.400. There are companion specifications, such as X.410 and X.430, that are necessary to implement if the X.400 mail service is to be successful. In the basic X.400 specification, two services are specified for the overall Message Handling System (MHS). The first type, Interpersonal Messaging System (IPS) is for messages serving interpersonal needs (such as what most users would consider electronic mail) as well as existing Telex and Telematic services already in use. The second model, Message Transfer (MT) serves a broader base (general, application-independent message transfer). Other standards specify specific implementation instructions for these two basic services:

a) X.401 lists the basic service elements and optional user facilities
b) X.408 specifies MHS conversion algorithms when manipulating data between different entities
c) X.409 defines the notational and representative techniques used to specify and encode MHS protocols
d) X.410 describes general MHS protocol techniques and the way in which OSI (X.200) protocols are used to support MHS operations
e) X.411 specifies protocols for the MT service
f) X.420 specifies protocols for the IPM service
g) X.430 describes how Teletex terminals can access MHS

In addition to being cognizant of what standard does what, it is important to point out that the various standards have set up methods in which messages are to be formatted in the standardized environment. Also, the X.400 service offering provides for division of groups (called domains) and appropriate management entities (administrators) in each group. Further, how does a network of mail managers keep track of who is on what machine? X.400 provides for directory servers to allow such management.

Even something as seemingly simple as electronic mail has some serious problems in the office environment. How are date and time stamps handled if the connection between offices transcends time zones or country barriers? What about language-sensitive prompts? All of these things must be considered in office automation when networks are concerned.

Other standards for office automation are starting to appear as well. ANSI and NISO are starting to propose international standards for file formats, image formats, specialized mail formats, and many other types of required file and communications formats necessary for the interconnection of office packages. These standards, coupled with IEEE, ANSI, and ISO network protocol and communications standards, will provide offices of the future with the needed connectivity between PCs, departmental computers, and corporate resources. Further, such connectivity will allow noncommunicating networks of today a method to connect and exchange office data.

Office Network Futures

Where are office networks going? Strange places, it seems.

Some vendors are experimenting with the use of infrared network connections to eliminate the need for office cabling. In this manner, the office can easily be reconfigured to accommodate many different office set-ups without the major headache of cabling and reconnection of existing and new devices on the network. While use of infrared may seem a little odd, in fact, infrared keyboard connections have been out a couple of years now and the network is a logical extension to such an arrangement.

Centralized wiring plants for offices are the rage at the moment. DEC has the DECConnect plan, IBM has theirs, AT&T has theirs, and so does practically everyone else. In all cases, the running of a few pairs or twisted pair seems to permeate all suggested cable plants, in addition to vendor-suggested coax, baluns, and God knows what else — all to the same connection plate in a wall. So while it is expected that new network technologies for the office will emerge in the short run, it is also expected that many of these technologies will make use of existing twisted pair cabling plants. Already there is a twisted pair Ethernet. ISDN runs over twisted pair as well. Token ring networks are also being moved to twisted pair. In short, offices will be in the twisted copper market for a while more, because it is inexpensive, easy to run, and supported at high speeds. It also makes sense for other reasons. Laptop computing is just getting on well and rumors abound about new generation laptops with incredible storage capabilities as well as display and access methods. With such capability in a portable format, the need to "plug in" to the network is critical and essential if office networks are to provide the services required by users of tomorrow.

Chapter Comments

Office automation and networks can coexist nicely. They need to. The office of today is going to change radically and the need for office and network connectivity will be essential. Concentration on network and office format standards as well as well-planned office strategies and networks will allow unsurpassed network connectivity for future offices.

Chapter Thirteen

Selecting Network Consultants

INTRODUCTION

In these days of tight budgets, getting the most for your money, get it done yesterday, fast-paced life of major league computing, the need to get information on the latest, faster and more efficient has become the way of life. We all want to make the "right " decision, but also want to do so in an educated, technically sound way. And, since our bosses think the world of us and know that we will lead them into successful paths of righteousness, we are the anointed few: Design, implement, and manage the new network.

Absolutely. Where do I sign?

Personally, I tend to get seriously concerned when management types start talking about networks. Since the big hoopla about the automated office began, networks have been a big deal as well. At first, management was concerned about office automation, but then they learned all about LOTUS 1-2-3 and figured out all the office automation buzzwords. Hence, they became experts at office automation. Now, as they say in beer commercials, it's network time. That means that management's next area to get involved in is the area of networks. This time, however, the problem is not as easy to solve as integration of a couple of office packages, nor is it as trivial as sticking a MODEM behind a PC. Don't get me wrong—I'm not slighting office automation. The point I'm illustrating is this: we all know that office automation is not trivial, but it is much easier to handle than the problem of networking; therefore, if management thinks they understand office automation (a lot think that they do), they're in for a BIG shock with networks. Most technical people don't understand networks, so true management enlightenment is still a long way off.

So, how do you find enlightened help in the design, implementation, and management of networks? Or, more simply put, how do you change water into wine? What is a Network Consultant?

Fear not, help is at hand. There is the elite corps of networking consultants, always eager to help and provide all the answers you need—for a fee, of course. But, before you go off and buy yourself a consultant, let's look into what a networking consultant is and what differentiates him or her from your basic computer consultant.

Networking consultants are a different type of computer consultant. Many computer consultants specialize in a given computer model: operating system, language, application area, or they are "generalists"—they know a little about a lot of things. Networking consultants have to be a little different. Not only do they have to understand operating systems, different computing hardware, languages, applications, etc., they also have to understand communications principles, hardware, software, troubleshooting, architecture, design, and many other things that many traditional computer consultants never have to get into. So, in brief, the networking consultant has to understand, in detail, both the hardware and the software of all the systems that the network will touch in addition to the customer's applications problems and business problems. They are hardware engineers, software engineers, architects, field service personnel, programmers, analysts, phone company analysts, and management consultants all wrapped up into one. A typical networking consultant will have at least five to ten years of network design and implementation, usually with multinode (system) networks (yes, Virginia, you can have a single node network) with networks ranging from two to 1,000 or more nodes. An important differentiation to note is that a node is a computer, not necessarily a terminal, printer, or other such "dumb" device. I'll get into why later. Also, networking consultants have exceptional communications skills (if you don't understand what they are trying to tell you, they're not much help), a good understanding of various network architectures, a good understanding of the various domestic and international standards (such as the ISO OSI model, various standards such as X.25, X.3, X.29,

X.21, V.35, EIA RS-XXX standards, IEEE standards, ANSI standards, etc.), insights into vendor developments, cable plants and layouts, tech control, network and system management, processor and I/O architecture, problem analysis abilities (if you can't define the problem, you can't solve it), programming experience with several languages (some lend themselves to communications programming better than others), and many other technical capabilities. The networking consultant should also possess the experience of a seasoned computer consultant and have experience with applications design and implementation.

If that weren't enough, the networking consultant should also understand system management, personnel management, budgeting and modeling, expansion analysis, project management, documentation procedures, policy analysis, design, and administration, short- and long-range planning, vendor interface techniques, and many other management-related skills. You should also consider other items such as educational background, customer base of the consultant (who else has he/she helped), professional society membership, and certifications. Certifications help take a lot of the guesswork out of selection, as the consultant will have had to pass an extensive test, submit credentials for review to a selection board, and, in most cases, sign an ethics statement. At present, there are three technical certifications of interest to anyone considering the hiring of a "certified" professional and all are offered and regulated by the Institute for the Certification of Computer Professionals (ICCP). These certifications are:

o **Certificate in Computer Programming (CCP).** This certification is geared towards professionals with a demonstrated capability in a selected computer language (or languages), programming methods, and other related topics. CCP is considered, usually, the most technical of all certifications but also the most narrow in terms of overall scope.

o **Certificate in Data Processing (CDP).** The CDP certification is a more generalized certification geared towards professionals with a demonstrated capability in various DP-related areas such as center management, DP procedures, system architecture, and other topics.

195

o **Certified Systems Professional (CSP).** Of the three certifications, the CSP is the newest. Started in 1984, the CSP designation was designed for professionals with a broad background in a variety of computer-related disciplines and is comprised of both highly technical and management-oriented topics. Items such as operations research, programming methods, MIS operations, networking, systems architecture, systems analysis, and many other topics comprise the list of requirements for earning the CSP.

In addition to passing a fairly comprehensive test for each certification, each certification requires that all professionals achieving certification recertify every three years through a plan of demonstrable continuing education in their field or through retesting. When hiring consultants, certification will become more and more critical as the network marketplace expands and requires that consulting professionals provide a standardized method of submitting credentials for customer approval.

Experience, Experience, Oh Wonderful Experience!

In all cases remember that there is no substitute for actual experience; all the academic courses and professional memberships in the world cannot replace being bitten by the network snake. Ask for references and call them for information on the networking consultant you have selected. Remember that you are most likely interrupting their work schedules, so keep your queries short and to the point. Things to ask about would be analytical capabilities (how long it took for the consultant to figure out the problem), quality of work, how long the consultant worked for the customer, would the customer hire the consultant again, and other questions along this vein. Be careful when asking about the nature of work that was done; many customers of consultants cannot discuss the company's networking set-up due to corporate policies and, in cases where the final product is being resold by the customer, the customer will not wish to discuss it, as it may put him or her in an embarrassing situation. You can find out what you need to make a decision without getting into the architecture of the networks of the consultant's clients.

By now, you are probably convinced that I have completely lost what marbles I had left. No, not yet. In a networking environment, the network consultant has the responsibility to his or her customer to provide the "right" solution, not just "a" solution. And, since the network will eventually touch the customer's business in most facets, the networking consultant has to have the experience and the insight to design and implement the network in a manner that the customer will be able to use and expand without redesigning the network and without incurring unnecessary costs. This usually requires drawing upon the skills in the above paragraph and in the tenacity of the consultant to provide a clear, unbiased solution to the problem at hand.

How to Best Utilize a Network Consultant

Well, we now know what qualifications a networking consultant should have. Let's look at the way you should use networking consultants to get the best mileage out of your consulting budget.

Rule number one in using a consultant: let the consultant HELP you make a decision based upon informed opinion, but, in all cases, make the final call yourself. You will be the one responsible, not the consultant, when everything blows up on Friday night at 5:00. If you let the consultant make your decisions for you, you can rest assured that you will be disappointed at some time or another. There are many consulting types in the marketplace, but truly enlightened consultants know better than to make decisions for the customer for a couple of reasons: the customer has to be comfortable in his or her decision to be satisfied with the implementation, and a consultant's role is NOT to make decisions; the consultant is there to present workable alternatives and give educated opinions based upon previous experience and understanding of the customer's needs. I've always told consultants that unless they can come up with at least three different ways to solve the same problem, they're not doing their jobs. Having the necessity of choice allows the customer to choose the "right" way to do the job based upon the business needs of the company, which the customer will always understand better than the consultant.

Rule number two in choosing a networking consultant: don't think that you can do it all yourself. You wouldn't be thinking about hiring a consultant if you could. Many times, consultants will recommend actions that may seem like a waste of time to you, but, in reality, are very necessary. A group I was involved with recently wanted to put in a very large network with PCs and systems scattered all over the western hemisphere. What they wanted was to do most of it themselves and have me provide guidance for them, which was fine. But, when it came time to look at the cost matrix and traffic matrix and compute both for the first phase of the network, they felt that the matrix computations were unnecessary because they weren't sure what the growth would be. I tried to convince them otherwise, but they did not want to hear anything other than their own words. At that point, I gave them their money back and walked away from the project. The reasons? Computation of the traffic matrix (how much data from what node to what node and how often for all nodes on the network) is critical to network design because it will dictate how much data can be shoved through the network before the performance dies. It also shows the load factors on the systems on the network that will be accessing the data involved. The traffic matrix also shows how much expansion room will be available and how long the current design will last before it has to be subdivided, enhanced, or replaced with a better design architecture. Second, the cost matrix is important, as it will dictate how much money will be necessary to transfer data between nodes. It is also useful in setting up the least cost path between nodes. So, without these two factors being computed, it is virtually impossible to wave the rubber chicken at the network and declare it functional and wonderful. While it is true that the customers may not have known what they would be expanding to, they did know what they currently had and could have set up a base from which to work. If you know the basic capabilities, you will also know how much you can expand before you have to do a major overhaul on the network. Also, if you have some idea as to how fast the business will expand (you can find this out through a historical perspective on the company's business), you can estimate how long it will be before the network reaches critical mass and something will have to be done. Therefore, how extensive a network will be or how much data it can/will handle is directly dependent upon a good estimate of traffic load and plugging in cost numbers.

A good consultant provides conservative, truthful answers to problems based upon actual, factual information, not rumors, estimates, or heresay that cannot be substantiated with facts. So, it may look like magic, but it isn't. Use the consultant for the hard stuff, have him or her suggest things that you can do on your own (to save you money and time), and remember that he or she is the person you hired because of his or her knowledge. Use it!

Good Consultants Are Truthful Consultants

Rule number three in selecting a networking consultant: a good consultant will always tell you the truth, no matter how unpalatable it may be. It is better to know what is real and will work than implement something that sounds good but won't. An experienced networking consultant will be able to help you differentiate between real and unreal and will not hesitate to point out the differences. If you know what is real, your disappointments will be few and your successes many.

Complexity Is Better Than How Many Nodes

Rule number four in selecting a networking consultant: the complexity involved in network designs the consultant has worked on is much more desirable than how many nodes. I've seen consultants who claimed 100 node networks and, after some research, the "network" turned out to be 100 terminals with 1200 baud MODEMs dialed up to a system, playing dumb terminals. That's distributed processing, which is not the same as networking. I'd rather use a consultant who has had to configure a network with local area linkages (such as Ethernet), configuration of routing nodes, gateways (to X.25, SNA and others), internets, repeaters, and other such items. That kind of practical experience with difficult connectivity problems is much more useful than how many nodes someone has hooked up to a wire or how many dial-ups there are on a computer.

Network Management Is a Must

Rule number five in selecting a networking consultant: look for experience in network use and management. Many consultants are quick to configure a network, but few have practical, daily experience in running a network and providing technical control and support of network resources. This is a critical item because management of a network leads to empathy with the customer—the problem is seen from the customer's side, as the consultant has been there before. There are some real problems in the support area of the network that have to be experienced to be believed, so look for a consultant with direct control experience. I always liken this item to the problem of dealing with vendor engineering. When I worked for a major computer vendor, I can remember producing solutions and software that were sound from an engineering standpoint, but the customers sometimes gave me grief because it was "not enough" or "too difficult to use" or, worse yet, they "didn't need all the features." As a consultant, I had a hard time figuring out what they wanted. However, when I was a customer in the same predicament, I understood immediately what it was they were talking about. Just because the engineering expertise is sound does not mean that a consultant understands all the aspects of the solution. Also, a good consultant is not afraid to bring in other help when out of his or her league. This means that it is much better to find a consultant who uses other personnel with different expertise than one who tries to do it alone. There is safety in numbers when it comes to design, and use of a knowledge base rather than a single individual increases the likelihood of a superior solution.

How Much Does a Consultant Cost?

Since you have found the ultimate consultant and are now ready to wage war on the network problem that has been confronting you, the question of the hour comes up: How much do networking consultants cost? Well, they ain't cheap.

Typical consulting rates for networking consultants usually run about 20-40 percent higher than comparable rates for straight computer consultants. Some rates are as low as $35 an hour and you can expect to pay as much as $250 an hour for top folks working on difficult problems. Some consulting firms charge flat rates per day ($500-$2,500 a day) and can also quote flat rates for projects that have been well defined. Remember, in all cases, you get what you pay for. You may pay $150 an hour for a top consultant, but you may only need him or her for a couple of weeks, whereas you may pay $50 an hour for a less experienced consultant and end up using him or her for two months. That is not to say that less expensive consultants are not as experienced, but most top consultants are in demand because of their experience and charge higher prices accordingly. Overall, if you consider the fact that a bad network put together without proper design can cost up to five times more to fix or replace than a properly designed and implemented network, the price of a good consultant is cheap. By the way, if you find a good networking consultant, hang onto him or her. They're not that easy to find.

When looking for a good consultant, there aren't many places to go for information, but there are some. User groups are good places to start. Yes, I know that many user groups are supposed to be noncommercial, but users will be users. Asking other user group members at local and national meetings can be a good way to find good consultants. Another method is to contact companies with networks and ask their networking managers for names of consultants. Vendors are usually a help in finding consultants as well, but beware: they will usually try to sell you their own personnel. Finally, contact professional computer membership organizations for help; they usually can provide names through a referral service or membership roster.

In summary, be selective in choosing a network consultant and remember, they can be very helpful in the design, implementation, and management of your network. It's like the old business adage "to make money, you have to spend money." Choose a consultant with a good track record, one you feel you can trust. And, always beware of the definition of GURU: "Good Understanding, but Relatively Useless."

Chapter Fourteen

Distributed Database Issues

INTRODUCTION

One of the problems of distributed processing is that the processors are all distributed. It would be nice if they were all in the same place so that when things broke and when things went nuts, all you had to do was walk down the hall and reboot the system. Users usually don't mind too much, especially after they recover from the initial shock (strokes have a way of taking the pep out of you). Unfortunately, distributed means just that and it also means that networked systems will probably be scattered all over the western hemisphere or across the globe.

For those who are snickering over the fact that all you have is a two-node network, keep it up while you can. Management has this funny habit of changing everything when you least expect it and it usually means more nodes, more work, same budget, less time. Sound familiar?

Along with the problem managing remote systems is the problem of remote user support. Frequently, on larger networks, there are no trained personnel to handle the remote system management needs and user assistance needs. Users usually have to fend for themselves and, as a rule, have a great deal of difficulty doing it. Ever try to explain to a user how to reboot a system? Try to explain to them how to switch the MODEM on the leased line into remote digital loopback. Now you are getting the picture.

To add insult to injury, with the increasing use of relational databases on corporate systems, the network manager is faced with the unpleasant task of supplying virtual terminal support to remote systems so that users may access the database or he/she has to figure out a way to allow access, remotely, to the database from any machine in the network. This is a difficult problem and is not trivial to solve; most vendors do not set up their database products to allow remote access, and many networking products do not provide virtual terminal access capabilities. Of course, they'll tell you anything, but delivery is a completely different matter.

By the way, if I sound a bit cynical when it comes to vendor claims concerning networks, I am. I've been burned so many times by vendor claims that I've taken out fire insurance on myself.

Now, as if you didn't have enough problems to deal with, management has deemed it necessary to put in an SNA network next to your bright, shiny DECnet network. How wonderful. And, since you have done so well with management of the DECnet network, and therefore, by implication, must be a wonderfully talented person (you probably are if you can get the silly thing to work right day after day), you get the honor of running the SNA network. Of course they trust you. Of course it has to talk to the DECnet network. Well, obviously, the ORACLE database on your VAX system has to talk to DB2 on the IBM. Isn't that what networks are for? By the way, you should be warned that the new VP of Finance will be installing a Prime 750 and will also need access to the current databases. Your job, whether you decide to accept it or not, Mr. Phelps, is to "get them networks talking to each other!"

The final problem has to do with management of tasks. Everyone has their own way of doing things and in companies without centralized systems management, it is not uncommon to see three or more different relational database products on the systems basically fulfilling the same functions. This usually happens over a period of time and, by the time a company is ready to "standardize" on a given database product or vendor, the users have written a great deal of applications that are database specific and would require a great deal of time to change over. You know — users. Those people who justify your existence. The same ones you keep the .357 in the upper lefthand drawer for (just in case one comes in with Hollerith cards). Those nice folks that caused the creation of the term "mental breakdown." Yep, the same ones that will refuse to learn the new database, do not want to change anything, and will fight you to the death over their right to use any software product they deem necessary to do their job, whatever it may be.

Management, God love 'em, has the perfect solution.

"You can do it, Mark! We have confidence in you! Just don't spend any money, hire any people, or cause any disruption in the way we do business. Other than that, do anything you need to get the job done. Also, we know that it will be difficult, but we will remember you generously at raise time next year if, we get the contract we've been working on and our profit margin is better than it is now."

What a spirit lifter! You, and you alone, have been selected to pull off the miracle of the century... OK, I'm exaggerating a little. Not much, but a little. Friends of mine can attest to this. I've been known to work a little magic from time to time, but alchemy is a little out of my league. Also, waving the rubber chicken at the network will not necessarily work either.

Therefore, how does one solve the problem of communication between systems attempting to access distributed databases on the various systems in the network?

The most logical solution is to use a "front-end" of sorts to "talk" to the databases and also to communicate across the network. This sounds pretty simple, but it is not that easy to do. Different networks have different ways to communicate task-to-task and different databases have different ways of parsing queries from users as well as different "languages" for querying the databases.

Within the structure of DECnet, there is the capability to allow task-to-task (program to program) communication between systems participating on the DECnet network. Basically, programs are written for each node (system) on the network and set up as a network task. After this is done, the program on the remote node is "connected to" and communications happen via network service routines, similar to file reads and writes. Once the work is complete, the user terminates the program on the host node and the link is destroyed.

While this technique allows one to access a type of network, it does not solve the problems of dissimilar networks and of query translation from database to database. So, for starters, let's look at the relational database problem.

Some relational databases, such as ORACLE (and, lately, INGRES) use a query language called SQL to access the database and also use SQL statements from programs to talk to the database kernel. As a result, programs passing SQL statements in the proper manner to routines from the database-callable library can access the database in a reasonable manner. Other databases, however, use different techniques to access the database. A Britton-Lee database machine expects the host to parse the query and pass database primitive information to it, not parse the query after it is received and pass the information back to the host. Other databases use variations such as QUEL, TEQUEL, and other home-grown methods (such as the Datatrievelike interface to Rdb/VMS) to communicate to the database kernel. The points being that: a) every database has its own routines to talk to the database kernel and b) some data bases parse the query in the subroutine and others parse the query in the database kernel.

The next, and more severe, problem is that of communicating to dissimilar networks. We have all heard of gateways ("portals" into different networks) and various vendors offer them as methods by which to communicate with dissimilar machines on other networking protocols. This is all well and good, but there are some significant drawbacks to this type of thinking. For one thing, it is not only necessary to have networking expertise for one kind of network; now it is necessary to have expertise for all types of networking protocols available for access. This gets very expensive and can be very scary. What happens when the network guru you hired leaves the firm? Now, the fireworks really start. Sure, you will survive, but it will be quite painful for a while. Also, finding good people with multinetwork expertise is very difficult. Just try it sometime. Compound these problems with the hassle of differing hardware, differing software, and the general hassles of support and maintenance and the problem becomes increasing clear: multivendor networks get very expensive very quickly.

As with all problems, there are solutions, and the multivendor network is no different. The basic problem that needs to be solved is the communication between dissimilar systems on a reasonable basis. The wrench in the solution is that there is no cohesive, standardized architecture that allows this to happen.

Contrary to anything that you may have heard, networking is still in its infancy stages. Most companies take the idea that one person or firm has developed and tend to copy it with their own implementation scheme. Hah, you say! Yes, they do. The final products may not look much like each other, but the basic rudiments are similar. For example, many networks use what is called the "circuit" concept of networking. This means that a remote system sets up a physical routing and virtual connection to a host on a network. This virtual connection exists until the remote or the host discontinues the session. During that time frame, both the host and the remote have to manage the link from both ends and are continually monitoring the status of transmissions and link activity. This happens for every connection to/from the nodes and can be a real pain to manage as well as debug and support. Another example is the token ring. Someone came up with the idea and next thing you know, there are slotted rings, bidirectional rings, etc. But, the basic element is the token and a ring; everyone else has their implementation of the basic idea.

Another situation is the use of "standardized" protocols. Sure, there is X.25, IEEE 802.3, RS232-C, and many others, but stop and consider this: 90% of the "standardized" protocol architectures only specify layers 1 and 2 of the seven-layer Open Systems Interconnect (OSI) architecture. The other 10% attempt to specify level 3, but not with much success. In any case, there is no standardized seven-layer network architecture available for usage, as no standardizing organization has ever gotten around to completing standardization procedures for the upper layers. The International Standards Organization (ISO) is starting to get into the act, but ANSI and CCITT are taking their own sweet time. What this means is that most users of networks have to rely upon vendor expertise in the implementation of networks and hope that they know what they are doing. But it also means that the vendor will most likely NOT provide his or her seven-layer architecture on other vendors' systems and will settle for providing rudimentary gateway access to dissimilar networks. So, for example, if you buy DECnet for your VAX system (most of this applies to all DEC systems, by the way), you can choose to use standardized protocols (such as X.25) for levels 1 and 2 or you can use DEC's protocols (such as DDCMP, CTERM, or others). From level 3 up, however, you use DECnet, which, of course, only runs on DEC operating systems on DEC machines (according to DEC). You could implement DECnet on an IBM mainframe, but if IBM changed the operating system or if DEC announced Phase V tomorrow, you could be dead in the water until you provided an upgrade to the software or hardware. To compound the problem, even if you did implement DECnet on another system, there are copyright questions to be answered as well as the problems of implementation. While DECnet provides general adherence to the map of the OSI model, the actual implementation is somewhat cryptic and is fraught with neat things like Ancillary Control Processes (ACPs) and other nifties that make implementation of DECnet on anything other than DEC operating systems very difficult (and somewhat difficult on some DEC operating systems). I should also mention that if you are industrious, it can be done. I got a version of DECnet up and running on my Macintosh a while back and I have seen such feats done on other operating systems by other folks as well. Therefore, implementation of a selected vendor's architecture on all machines on a network is worthwhile, provided you have the ability to support it and the architecture provides the necessary functionality.

One of the main problems in the distributed database environment is the issue of what is called database transparency. Database transparency refers to the issue of a user accessing a relation in a given database on any node without having to specify the node. The net effect is that access to the database and the included relation is transparent to the user and he/she does not know that there is a network involved in getting to the database. Some vendors, such as DEC, have already implemented this capability to an extent. For instance, in Rdb/VMS, it is possible to INVOKE (open) a database on a remote node (provided DECnet is available between the systems) and access the relations in the database as if they were local. The problem of data transparency becomes worse as multiple nodes may have multiple databases, which contain multiple relations. How does one keep track of all this information in a manner that everyone knows where everything is and not kill the systems and network in the process? Also, what about the problem of accessing multiple relations in dissimilar databases on various nodes simultaneously, such as a multirelation, multinode CROSS (JOIN) operation? This is a highly desirable feature that no vendor has implemented to date and with good reason: it is a very difficult software engineering problem to solve.

Another issue with distributed databases comes with the problem of knowing when the data has been "committed" or stored properly in the database. In the distributed environment, it is necessary for the sending node to tell the user or the program that the data was sent and then receive not only an acknowledgment back from the remote node's networking software that the packet was received but also an acknowledgment from the remote database that the data was correctly and safely stored in the remote node's database or relation. The technique that is used to provide this function is called a two-stage commit (stage one is on the host and stage two on the remote node), one that is implemented in very few so-called "distributed" databases. A two-stage commit is essential if multiple databases being accessed across a network are to be entrusted with any type of data that requires reliability.

As with any network application, the problem of data transfer speed and access time is always an issue. In the distributed database environment, transfer speed can be a real issue. Suppose a user on a MicroVAX II decides to copy a 200Mbyte relation over to his or her node from the clustered 8600? All things being optimal, there could be a great deal of traffic involved, not to mention the problem of how to keep users from killing the network with unnecessary data transfers. Consider, also, the up-and-coming problem of CD-ROMs on PC's. What if the CD-ROM contained, say, a 300Mb database and a user decided to copy sections of it into the VAXCluster database? What if there were more than one user doing it at a time? You begin to see the problem.

The benefits of distributed databases far outweigh the costs, as now applications dollars are saved, vendor independence is possible (utilizing front-end technologies), network gateways are reduced or eliminated, and distributed systems are easier to implement. Most importantly, manpower is reduced (if all systems are running the same networking software, there is no cross-network experience factor necessity) from a network support point of view and the use of advanced application building tools allows the user, not a programmer, to develop his or her own applications. Remember, the most expensive component in any system or network is not the hardware — it's the brainware of the people who have to program and support the applications, systems, and network.

Obviously, there is nothing yet on the market to do such a feat. Some companies have taken it upon themselves to use a vendor-supplied networking architecture and try to provide some capabilities themselves, but this is mostly a limited effort and does not really solve the problem. I know of a company that is working on such an interface, but as with all good things, it takes time. What is important is to differentiate what is a REAL distributed database from the fakes. Truly distributed databases should provide the following basic capabilities:

- o Two-stage commit
- o Node transparency (the user should not have to know what node the information resides within)
- o Network product transparency (it should not matter if the network used is Ethernet, token ring, DECnet, or SNA)

o Multinode simultaneous access (users should be able to have multiple databases open on multiple nodes simultaneously)

o Ability to use relational operators on multiple OPEN databases and multiple relations simultaneously (i.e., a JOIN operation from multiple relations in multiple databases in multiple nodes)

o Multinode journaling, rollback, and recovery

o Application transparency (an application should not have to be modified or recoded to take advantage of the distributed database capability)

o Multinetwork architecture capability (most companies to not support only DECnet or only SNA; there is usually a mixture of multiple networking technologies)

o Identification of query requests that will require a large amount of data transfer over the network and allow the user to confirm or deny the request before the network gets buried

o Access path "memory" (queries that are sent off to remote nodes that are similar to previous query paths should not have to thrash around in an indexing scheme more than necessary)

o Network access statistics and network usage statistics should be integral to the distributed access capability to help in monitoring actual network usage by the database, perform timing tests, monitor system and network performance, and to provide heuristic, historical information to management when more powerful machines or networking capabilities are required

o Integrated set of database and network monitoring and management tools

Something that I don't necessarily view as required but something I view as being highly desirable would be the ability to access dissimilar databases (such as Rdb/VMS, Oracle, or Ingres) with a single query. This, obviously, would require a type of "query translator," but it would be very useful to companies with dissimilar database technologies on dissimilar machines.

The point that I would like to make clear is that distributed relational databases are the trend of most companies in the future and will be necessary to provide management timely information while not centralizing all the database horsepower in one location. Those of you who are giggling again better look out. That user down the hal l with DBASE III may be your boss someday and require that all databases on PCs be connected to the mainframe. Why? Because marketing information for 10 different regions are on those PCs and the corporate twinkies want an update as to what is going on, but they don't want to dictate to the regions how to do their work. Still giggling? I've already gotten requests for such nonsense, so if you don't hear anything yet, just wait a while — it's coming.

Getting a distributed database up and running is not easy and is heavily dependent upon the network(s) and relational databases that you will be using. For those with networks and relational databases, the day is coming. For those with no network but relational databases, your time is coming as well. And for the rest of y'all out there, beware: vendors are getting their relational databases up and running on PCs, so the herd of relational databases in a company is a very real possibility. So, the time that your manager comes in with the idea that he would like you to connect all the relational databases in the company together, remember the .357 is in the upper lefthand drawer of your desk.

Chapter Fifteen

Network Training

INTRODUCTION

How many times have you received educational junk mail in your office in-basket? If you are like me, it is a pretty regular occurrence. As a matter of fact, I tend to believe that educational courseware promotional brochures account for over half the use of paper in the world today, but that is another story for another time. Out of those brochures, more and more companies are pushing network and network-related courses as part of their offerings (I know this because I see the same companies sending me networking brochures with the same instructors on them as the courses on introductory systems courses). Even the big boys, such as Digital, are spending more money and time getting their network course curricula developed to help meet the needs of the "exploding network marketplace."

I'm all for professionally made and delivered courses. As a matter of fact, I've developed quite a few myself and I have also delivered, literally, hundreds of seminars on a variety of subjects (particularly networks). I have noticed, however, that there are some areas that many folks never address when considering network education that are critical to understanding what is being received for the money spent. Like any good consumer, we all try to get the best value for the money spent. In these days of tight travel and educational budgets, it is even more critical that training we receive is what we need and of a quality that is useful to us when we return to the job. Therefore, in this article we shall explore network training: how it "happens," what to look for, who needs it, and how much does it cost.

One of the first things to remember in any course that you may attend is the problem of course development. Have you ever seriously thought about the work and effort that goes into development of a course or, more importantly, what caused the course to be developed to start with? Well, it starts, usually, with market research. An enterprising company or individual identifies a need for network education, identifies a target marketplace, figures out how much money can be made, and presents his or her case to company management. If the marketing metrics are good, the company will typically identify course development resources, identify course developers, course instructors, set up a development schedule, and set up a course pilot delivery schedule to test the new course on potential consumers. When the course is developed and completed its testing (the pilot courses), final modifications and enhancements are made, the final handouts and labs produced, copies are made of all materials, and courses are scheduled for delivery to consumers. Obviously, this is an abbreviated list of actions that take place, but it is easy to get the picture that course development, professionally done, takes time and effort and a great deal of resources.

Probably the toughest part of the course development cycle is finding a competent courseware developer for the network subject that has been identified. While it is true that there are a great many individuals who are competent network professionals, the real problem with network training is the issue of how to impart a networking professional's knowledge and experience into a new consumer in a reasonable and expedient fashion. Development of a course is not like delivering, or instructing, a course. The developer has to be acutely aware of how to present concepts, facts, and issues in a manner that both the instructor can present to the students and also so the students can understand the material from the instructor as it is presented. Therefore, a course developer has to have a unique set of qualifications if a course is to be successful. He has to be very knowledgeable (or develop the knowledge, but that takes more time) in the subject presented, know how to write for the consumer, understand the problems and concepts of educating students and instructors, plan lesson time according to content and what can be reasonably learned in the planned time frame, and, most importantly, be able to impart knowledge and experience to the student in a manner in which the student can use the knowledge gained when he/she returns to the job.

Now for reality. In many larger companies, the previously described methods of course development is the standard methodology used. Many times, however, companies interested in the "quick kill" or the ones that jump on the network bandwagon do not follow good, standardized course development procedures. The results can be catastrophic for everyone involved. I've attended courses where the instructors did not know how to teach their subject or did not have any idea as to what they were teaching, either because the course was not developed properly or the instructor was not familiar with the subject being presented. One time, years ago, I attended a seminar on network queueing theory that got me so confused that it took me four months to get myself straightened out and then I found out what I had "learned" was WRONG!! Boy, was I hacked! I spent a good deal of time trying to explain what I learned to my coworkers, some of which did not understand what I was relaying (thank goodness — that was my first sign that something was amiss) to them as a result of the course. Others knew enough about the subject to let me know that something was not right about what I had been told. I then went in a search for truth and found that I had been misled. It proved to be very embarrassing for me, for my coworkers, and, ultimately, for the company that ran the course (to say I caused them some grief would be a gross understatement). After all was said and done, a badly developed course with a poor instructor caused a great deal of problems and ended up costing valuable productivity time not to mention wasted software due to the need to redesign and recode sections when the truth was later discovered. So, reality is that there are very good courses offered by both large and small companies. There are also very bad ones as well.

Now that we have seen how courses are developed, let's consider instructor qualifications for a bit.

I'm a firm believer that experience is the best teacher in the world. While it is true that college has a lot to offer, in the area of network education, most college's curricula leave a great deal to be desired. As a result, many colleges do not have good, solid educational offerings in network subjects and many emphasize the theoretical aspects of networking instead of the practical aspects. Don't get me wrong — I'm not knocking college education. There are some very fine colleges who offer excellent networking courses, but there are usually very difficult to get into and run on a semester basis, something not very conducive to productivity in the workplace. Therefore, most competent networking instructors and consultants I have met have developed their practical competence through the trial-and-error method and have been smart enough to learn from both their successes and their mistakes as well as those that others have experienced. Through the education through experience path, many things come to light in network education such as the problems that are not in the documentation, the problems of politics, the problems of dissimilar network software versions on different machines, and many other problems that can be very subtle and very confusing. Anyone can read a manual — experienced people know this very well. What makes a good networking instructor is one who not only has read the manual, but has had to implement what the manuals say, what they don't say, and also had to violate the rules to get the network to work. There is no substitute for experience and the best networking instructors have a lot of it, know how to teach it to their students, and understand the issues of how to apply it in the real world on real problems.

Some instructors know how to teach but do not necessarily understand the subject that they are teaching. As a matter of fact, some larger training companies have, historically, hired experienced educators (such as high school teachers) and taught them the subject matter so that they, in turn, could teach the subject to the students who attend the course. This technique can work very well on low-end (introductory) courseware where questions are usually not very complex and are related to the subjects presented. In more technical courses, however, the instructor really needs to be experienced for the students to get the most out of the course that they are attending. In my experience, I often find that students in the more technical courses are attending the course to find out information on the presented subject. Very often, however, they are there to ask pointed questions about applications and networks they are working on and to draw from the instructor's expertise. If the instructor is not capable of helping the advanced student out, the student usually feels somewhat dissatisfied with the course or feels that the course did not meet the student's needs. Both of these will cause the ratings of the course to drop as well as the instructor's teaching ratings. As a result, the course may have been in line with the course description and may have covered the networking topics described, but such was not done to the satisfaction of the student, therefore, the course was not satisfactory as far as the student was concerned. Experience can make the difference, especially in high-end (very technical) courseware, as to whether the course will be successful or not in the eyes of the consumer, the student.

What about course content?

Every networking course that is developed has a topic list that is usually included in any marketing literature that is sent out about the course. Things to look for include a clear, thorough outline of course topics to be covered, a brief description of the course (a management-oriented overview), a section that describes WHAT will be learned at the course, PREREQUISITES for the prospective attendee, WHO will be teaching the course, HOW LONG the course will last, and HOW MUCH the course costs. Beware of courses that do not include an outline or do not seem to give a clear idea on what is taught. Also, some courses may have more than one instructor listed but, in the fine print of course, a statement is usually made that not all instructors will be present at each course offering or location. Sometimes, no instructor is listed at all. This is not necessarily bad, but you should check to see who is teaching the course and what their expertise is before attending to insure that you will be satisfied with the instructor and the delivery of the course. I liken course attendance to going to the doctor. I much prefer to go to a doctor who is a specialist when I have a particular problem (such as a sprained ankle) and know who that person is and what kind of experience he/she has so that I can feel confident that I am spending my money properly and getting the best value for my cash. Also, one does not go to an optometrist to get a sprained ankle taken care of. So, specialization helps identify the right individual for the job. Network instructors need to have a wide base of experience, but they should always have an emphasis on networks. Companies that offer network training that are serious networking education companies will offer a variety of networking courses from the introductory level through to the very technical level. This is a good sign as it shows that they are seriously committed to network education and have attacked the network education problem at all levels. It usually can indicate, especially with smaller companies, that there is a good deal of expertise available within the company and that the introductory courses will be just as useful as the technical courses. Companies that provide training in "strings," groups of course offerings from the introductory range in a subject through to the advanced area, are seriously committed to education in that subject and are trying to provide a range of solutions for prospective consumers.

Facilities for network courseware can cause an interesting problem. If you have noticed pricing, network courses tend to be more expensive than "comparable" courses in operating systems or other subjects. This is due to a variety of reasons. To develop networking courses and expertise requires a network (or multiple networks). This means that the cost is much greater, in terms of components necessary, than developing courseware that can be done on a single machine. Networking courses that offer lab sessions cost more because single machine networks are tough to work with and multiple machines, which is what a network consists of, cost a lot more. When looking into network course offerings and a lab is offered, ask questions about the lab conditions and what kind of network resources will be available for learning AT THE LOCATION YOU WILL BE ATTENDING THE COURSE!!! Many times brochures can be somewhat misleading. Resources are claimed to be available and are — at some locations. Not all networking courses require lab time, but for those that do be sure you understand the facilities that will be available for use. Companies that offer full spectrum course offerings are usually a good bet as they need solid lab facilities to support their offerings. I've attended some networking seminars where the machines were brought in to the hotel where the seminar was being held, so it is quite possible that the claimed facilities will be available. Always check first.

Network courseware costs usually vary according to how many days the course will require to complete, where the course is being held, what facilities are necessary to support the course, how popular the course is, and how much overhead is incurred by the company providing the course. A popular course given by a popular instructor can sometimes be cheaper, as more students will attend each offering, increasing the profitability of the course and lowering the overall cost to the consumers. Low-end courses, such as introductory networking courses, usually last 2-3 days 3and can cost anywhere from $200.00 to over $700.00. Longer courses (3-5 days) can cost up to $1000.00. The more technical the course, the more it will cost. For instance, a five-day intensive introduction course may cost $1000.00, but a five-day internals course can easily cost $1500.00 or much more (up to $5000.00 per person per week). Technical courses require a lot more time and expertise to develop, so they tend to be more expensive. They also, typically, do not draw as many students over the life of the course as the low end courses and therefore cost more to recoup the development and overhead costs associated with the course.

Some companies that get networks (or will be getting networks) provide in-house education to their employees by contracting with outside educational vendors for courseware. Many times educational courseware vendors provide such courses at a substantial discount to a company because the overall overhead is reduced and a guaranteed student load is realized. Another important point is that travel costs for ten students can be substantial and bringing in a course can usually reduce the cost of education substantially. Many larger companies have known this for years, but smaller companies are starting to realize savings through on-site education as well. There are some other tangible benefits. Most of the time, a customer of an education vendor can specify certain topics to be covered and can also, where possible, specify a particular instructor. This can be very useful, as many times an experienced instructor can not only help educate a company's employees, but also provide customized network education for a given network environment as well as some on-site assistance as the course is being taught. I taught a networking course for a real estate appraisal company about seven years ago and quickly found out that the network was not even up and running yet and that they were having some serious troubles getting it operational. During breaks and when labs were scheduled, I spent my time working on the network and at the end of the week the students understood the network and it was up and running properly. Looking back on it now, they got a really good deal! I know since then, however, that most reputable and sincerely interested instructors will always spend time working with client companies to try to help them solve problems that arise during the progress of the course the instructor is delivering. I have one customer that has me teach a four-day course for them on a regular basis and always keeps me the fifth day to help them solve problems that have arisen since my last visit. So, good instructors, when teaching on-site, can provide expertise that is very useful in solving problems during the education process.

Now we have examined how courses are developed, who teaches them, what to look for in literature, facilities issues, and how much they cost. The question that now arises is: How do you know which network course you need to satisfy your needs?

The easy answer is that it depends upon your expertise. How you define your expertise will have a lot to do with how satisfied you will be with a seminar choice that you make. I've taught network product internals courses where some people who attended had never seen the product or had never seen a network. While I first thought that it was a fluke, I find that I run into it too often for it to be an anomaly. Two problems occur when you attend a course that is too advanced for your level of expertise: a) you will not understand what is being presented to you well enough to make efficient use of what you learn and b) you will hold up the entire class, which hurts everyone involved. Yes, it is true that most people will learn some things of use when they attend a course, no matter how advanced the course is over their level of expertise. It is also true, however, that retention of learned material degrades quickly if the material is not put into use soon after the learning process, so you end up losing most of what you gained, if any gain was made at all. When selecting a course of instruction on networks, be very honest in your self-appraisal of your expertise so that you can properly map the type of courses that you will require for your job. Another thing — never, ever attend more than one course at a time. Attending courses week after week does nothing but slow down the education process and reduce your learning and potential productivity. Always try to attend a course, wait about two months and experiment with the gained knowledge, and attend the next. This will insure maximum productivity for your training expenditure.

As a general guideline, the following sample job types will require network education as described:

- o Department Manager
  - Introductory course in networking
  - Introductory courses on networking products for which you have responsibility
  - Course on understanding network management
  - If you control PBX operations, look for the following seminar types:
    + PBX introductory courses
    + PBX planning and sizing
    + Cable management and planning
  - Networking trends and technology courses

- o Network Manager
  - Network product usage courses on networking products for which you have responsibility
  - Network management courses on networking products for which you have responsibility
  - Network programming courses on networking products for which you have responsibility
  - Courses on cable management and planning
  - Courses on network troubleshooting and debugging
  - Courses on network design and planning
  - Network architecture courses

- If you control PBX operations, look for the following seminar types:
  + PBX introductory courses
  + PBX planning and sizing
  + Cable management and planning
  + Specific courses on PBXs in use and under your control:
    o Programming
    o Managing
    o Implementing
    o Expanding
- Networking trends and technology courses

o Network Programmers
  - Network product usage courses on networking products for which you have responsibility
  - Network programming courses on networking products for which you have responsibility
  - Designing applications for networked environments
  - Network management conceptual courses
  - Network architecture course

o Network Users
  - Introductory course in networking
  - Introductory courses on networking products for which you have responsibility
  - Network product usage courses on networking products for which you have responsibility
  - Courses on how to use applications that have been developed or are in use in your environment

Obviously there are more job types than the above-listed ones, but you can get a fairly good idea of the level of education necessary for certain jobs. By the way, the job type of network manager assumes that the network manager already knows quite a bit about networks and the job type of network programmer assumes that the individual is already a competent programmer.

In summary, select network training just like you would select a system or any add-on component: carefully, weighing the advantages and disadvantages, and deriving maximum benefit for the cost and energy invested.